Y0-FDH-996

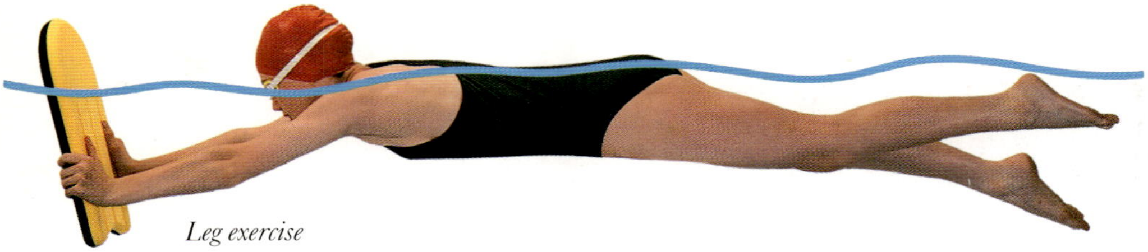

Leg exercise

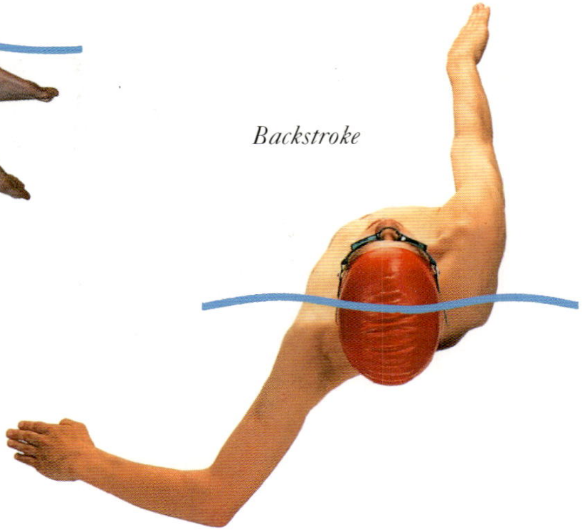

Backstroke

Synchro shape

Kneeling dive

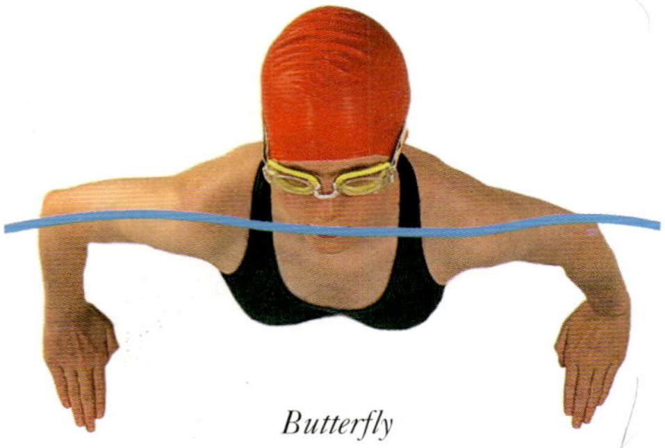

Butterfly

Star shape

Breaststroke turn

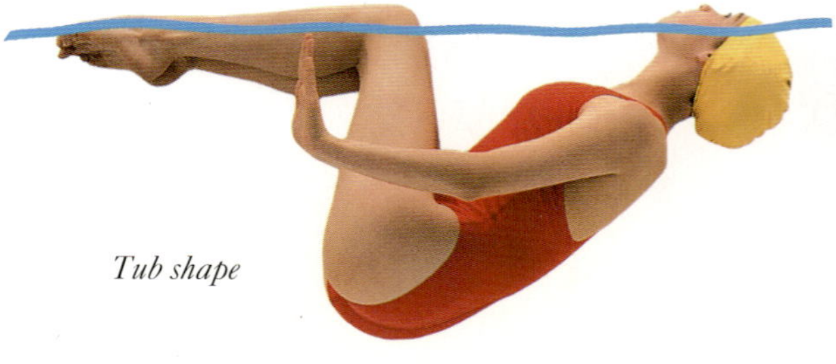

Tub shape

J. SPORTS
SWIMMING
ROUSE

THE YOUNG SWIMMER

JEFF ROUSE

Adjusting goggles

Ready to swim

PROPERTY OF
CLIFFSIDE PARK, PUB. LIB.

Alternating arms

Forward somersault

The crawl

DK

A DK PUBLISHING BOOK

Project Editor Lee Simmons
Design Penny Lamprell
DTP Designer Almudena Díaz
Picture Research Mollie Gillard
Production Josie Alabaster
US Editor Kristin Ward
Managing Editor Jane Yorke
Managing Art Editor Chris Scollen
Photography James Jackson
Swimming Consultant Rick Cross

The young swimmers
Harry Bond, Annabelle Halls, Marvin Jones, Jun King, Greta McLachlan,
Lisa Morrison, Laura Mulford, Kaya Ramjee, Melanie Stables

First American Edition, 1997
2 4 6 8 10 9 7 5 3 1
DK Publishing, Inc.
95 Madison Avenue, New York, New York 10016

Copyright © 1997 Dorling Kindersley Limited, London

Visit us on the World Wide Web at http://www.dk.com

All rights reserved under International and Pan-American Copyright Conventions.
No part of this publication may be reproduced, stored in a retrieval system, or transmitted
in any form or by any means, electronic, mechanical, photocopying, recording, or otherwise,
without the prior written permission of the copyright owner.
Published in Great Britain by Dorling Kindersley Limited.

A catalog record for this book is available from the Library of Congress.

ISBN 0-7894-1533-X

Color reproduction by Colourscan, Singapore
Printed and bound in Italy by L.E.G.O.

Contents

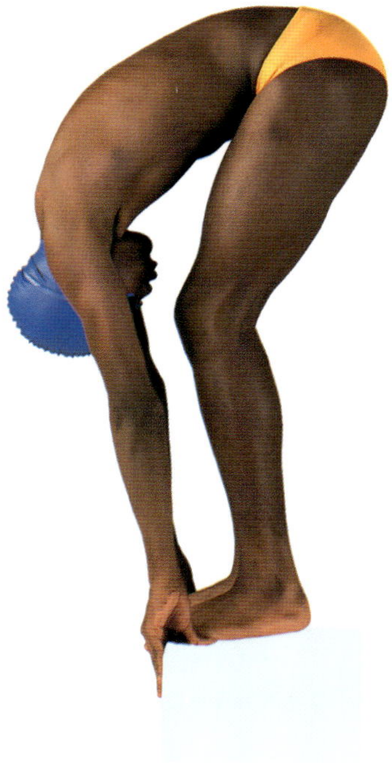

"Participation in the Olympics was always a dream of mine, so with a gold around my neck all I can say is 'thumbs up' to a dream come true!"

To all young swimmers

NO MATTER who you are or where you live, swimming is a rewarding activity to learn. This sport can provide you, as it did me, with the skills necessary to propel you through life; goal setting, time management, work ethic, and self-confidence are several of these important qualities. Swimming is a full-body exercise that provides you with excellent physical conditioning. But swimming is fun too, as anyone can tell you who has spent the afternoon floating, splashing, and playing in the pool. Confidence in the water can also lead to other endeavors such as water polo, water-skiing, scuba diving, and surfing. I hope that after reading this book you will appreciate how exciting and enriching swimming can be as a hobby, or a career.

"The home stretch of any race never looks easy!"

Jeff Rouse

"The start of a race is my first opportunity to shine so I make sure my form and focus is sharp!"

"Believe it or not, I have a great time during workout!"

"After this great swim in Phoenix, Arizona in 1996, I knew I was one step closer to winning an Olympic gold medal."

History of swimming

ANCIENT CARVINGS found in the Middle East suggest that people have been able to swim for over 4,000 years. Swimming began as a survival skill, and only really became popular as a sport in the 19th century. Early strokes included the breaststroke, sidestroke, and various forms of the crawl. The butterfly was the most recent stroke to be invented. It was used in breaststroke races until 1952, when it became an event in its own right.

Swimming with pig bladders
This stone frieze from ancient Iraq, dating from 869 BC, shows warriors crossing a river using inflated animal bladders and breathing tubes. The arm action is quite similar to that used in the crawl.

A popular pastime
Swimming was very popular in the early 19th century. Changing rooms lined the edges of the pool and swimming was segregated into men or women only.

Weissmuller went on to become a film star, starring as Tarzan.

Johnny Weissmuller
Weissmuller was one of the most famous American swimmers. In the 1928 Olympics he won nearly all the sprint titles. Because of improved methods of communication, his swimming actions were recorded, studied, and copied around the world.

Mark Spitz
At the 1972 Olympic Games in Munich, Germany, US swimmer Mark Spitz established himself as one of the greatest swimmers of all time. During the games he won seven individual events, all in world record time. He also swam in three team relay events.

Spitz at the 1972 Olympics. During his career he set 26 world records.

A man's typical swimsuit, 1921

Printed stripes improve the flow of water over the body.

The close-fitting Acquablade legsuit is for men and women.

Swimsuit design
Swimsuits have come a long way since the beginning of the century. Then, swimsuits were made of wool and were cumbersome and heavy. Today, advances in technology have resulted in fabrics that help to make swimmers more streamlined so they can improve their speed.

Starting to swim

TO START OUT in swimming all you really need is a swimsuit and a towel. However, if you plan to swim regularly with a team you will also need some of the items shown here. A sweatsuit, or other warm clothing, pool shoes, a cap, and goggles are important. Later, your coach might suggest using equipment such as kickboards and pull buoys. Ask your coach about the kind of food you should eat. You should certainly consider using a plastic drinking bottle if you start training sessions.

A cap makes you more streamlined in the water.

Swimmers wear swimsuits two sizes too small to streamline their bodies.

An extra towel may come in handy during training sessions or when attending swimming events.

Swimsuit

To cut down on drag in the water it is important that your swimsuit is the correct size and fits snugly. Most teams have their own team outfit in the team's colors, which members can buy.

Joining a team

Join a team to get expert advice on how to improve your swimming skills, and also to get the opportunity to take part in competitions. Inquire at your local pool or write to your nearest swimming association (see page 37) for information. Visit a team and watch the coaches at work to see what a training session involves.

Sweatsuit
Wear your sweatsuit to keep warm before and after training and also between swimming events at competitions. Your sweatsuit should be loose and comfortable.

Caps make it easy to identify team members in the water.

A swimsuit with a close-fitting high neck cuts down on drag.

Keep a plastic drink bottle handy in your bag.

Always change into pool shoes when at the pool since outdoor shoes are unhygienic.

You can store clothing and other equipment in a bag.

Basic equipment
Your coach will help you decide what equipment you need.

Pull buoys
These two types of pull buoys are specially designed for arms-only work. They fit lengthwise between your legs, just above your knees.

Handholds

Kickboards
Kickboards are useful buoyancy aids for legs-only work. They will help you improve your technique if you are starting out. If you already swim, they can help you strengthen your legs.

Paddles and mitts
Use hand paddles or hand mitts for extra arm strengthening work. Make sure they are the correct size for your hands.

Hand paddles

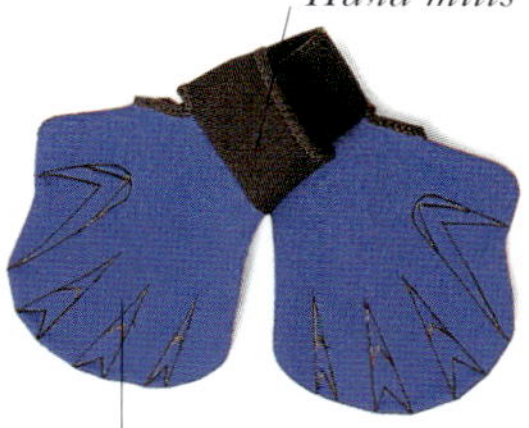

Hand mitts

The flexible material enables you to change your hand shape.

Weighted dive rings
Dive for rings to practice swimming underwater with your eyes open.

Chamois towel
A chamois towel is very absorbent, drying you quickly and efficiently.

Nose clips stop water from going up your nose.

Goggles
Goggles will protect your eyes from pool chemicals and will help you see more clearly in the water.

1 To put goggles on safely, hold the eyepieces on your eyes with one hand and hold the strap with the other.

Tuck loose ends of elastic into headstrap.

2 Stretch the strap over the back of your head and position it comfortably just above your ears.

Where to swim

SWIMMING IS THE perfect way to have fun, and stay in shape. All you need is a safe place to swim, such as your local pool. You can take swimming lessons here, or join a local team. Pools have changing rooms, lockers for your clothes and valuables, showers, footbaths, and lifeguards. Many pools have sides higher than the water level. Others are called "deck level" because the water washes over the edges. Competition pools are usually 164 ft (50 m) long with diving wells.

Open-water swimming

Ocean and open-water swimming and other water sports are very enjoyable, especially if you follow basic water safety rules. Make sure you can swim well and don't go swimming alone. Learn the meaning of warning flags and buoys. Ask lifeguards about the water conditions and read any warning signs that are posted.

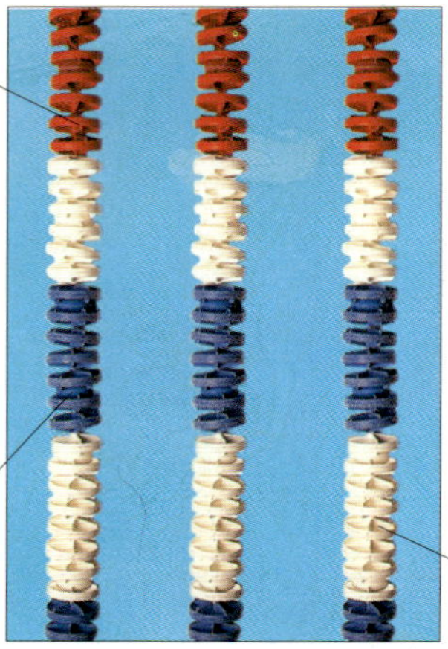

Lane lines

Lane lines are used to stop people from swimming into each other's paths. Some are called antiwave lines because the disks stop waves, or backwash, from spreading into another swimmer's lane.

Outdoor pools

While many international venues are indoors, some countries with a warm climate have open-air pools. The 1991 European Championships were held at this outdoor pool in Athens, Greece. Here, a training session for the event is in progress.

Competition pools

This picture shows Ponds Forge, in Sheffield, England. As with some competition-size pools, it has movable bulkheads at each end, so the length can be adjusted from 82 to 164 ft (25 to 50 m). The pool also has an adjustable floor so that it can be used for a large variety of swimming competitions, water polo, or synchronized swimming.

Diving rules

Diving into the water head first can be very dangerous, so it's important to follow certain rules.

- DO take notice of pool depth markers.
- DO go through the proper learning stages with your coach before diving.
- DO NOT attempt a racing dive in water less than 6 ft (1.8 m) deep.

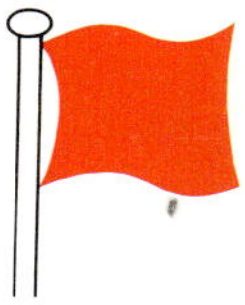

Warning signs

Warning signs, such as flags and boards, can be seen posted by lifeguard stations and along the beach. They designate the areas you can or cannot swim in.

Water safety

- Always tell someone where you are going and when you expect to be back.
- Keep a lookout for hidden obstacles under the surface.
- Get out of the water if you start to feel cold.

Nutrition

A car can't run without the right fuel and neither can you! You must eat well in order to give your body energy.

- Eat well before a competition.
- Eat soon after a competition to replace lost energy.
- Drinking fluid, such as water, is essential. Drink a little at a time, but often.

Backstroke flags

Flags strung across the pool 16 ft (5 m) from each end warn backstroke swimmers that the pool end is near.

164-ft (50-m) pool

Spectator stands

Diving wells have a minimum depth of 11.5 or 16 ft (3.5 or 5 m), depending on the board heights.

Diving boards of different heights

Competition officials stand by the lanes and check the timing, finishing order, and whether finishes are legal.

Starting block

For safety reasons, blocks with non-slip fiberglass tops are attached to the poolside. The top slopes down to the front to help swimmers dive off smoothly. Speakers are inserted into the blocks so that all the swimmers hear the starting signal at the same time.

Rails used for backstroke starts

Leisure pools

Some pools are leisure, or fun, pools. These have features such as wave-making machines and long, spiraling slides or chutes, called flumes. Flumes are made slippery by constantly running water.

Basic know-how

IF YOU ARE JUST starting out in swimming, trying these floating and gliding exercises will increase your confidence in the water. Start with the mushroom float, then try out different shapes, such as the star float or horizontal float. Floating and making different shapes on your front or back will show you how the shape you make in the water affects your balance.

Cheat at the beginning, by gently paddling with your hands.

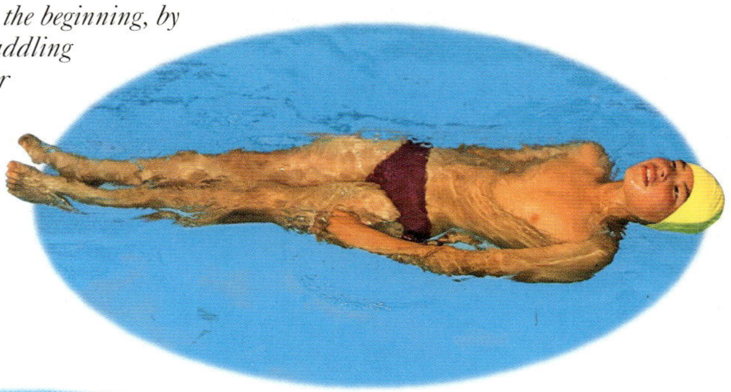

Horizontal float
Try to get your body as level as possible with the surface, with your head just resting in the water.

Star float
Stretch out on the surface as if you were lying on a clock face with your arms at about 10 o'clock and 2 o'clock and your feet at about 4 o'clock and 8 o'clock. If you find the float difficult, try it on your front first. Keep your head level with your body.

Mushroom float
This float is sometimes called a jellyfish float. It is a good exercise to start with if you are trying to float for the first time. Take a deep breath, lower your face into the water, then tuck your legs in tightly and hug them close. After sinking a little, you will gradually rise to the surface.

Floating
Breathe in and out very gently so that your lungs stay full of air and keep you afloat.

Push and glide on your front

Push and glide is a useful skill to learn as it encourages you to stretch out and find the most efficient body position for gliding.

Push and glide
These skills will help when you begin to learn starts and turns.

Keep your head down.

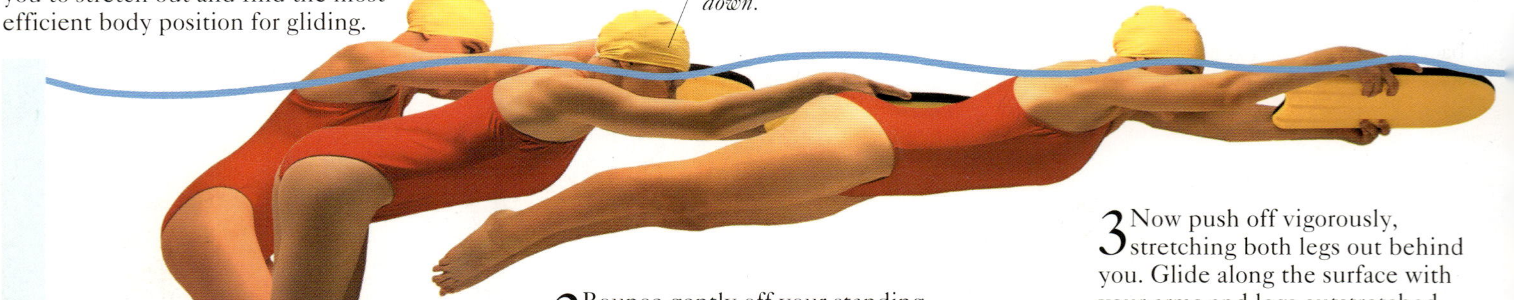

1 Stand with your back to the wall. Place one foot firmly against it and bend your other leg slightly. Stretch out your arms and hold on to the front of the kickboard, with your thumbs on top.

2 Bounce gently off your standing leg and place both feet side by side on the pool wall.

3 Now push off vigorously, stretching both legs out behind you. Glide along the surface with your arms and legs outstretched and your face in the water.

Hands on top
Another way to hold the kickboard is to put your hands over the leading edge and rest your arms lightly on the upper surface of the kickboard.

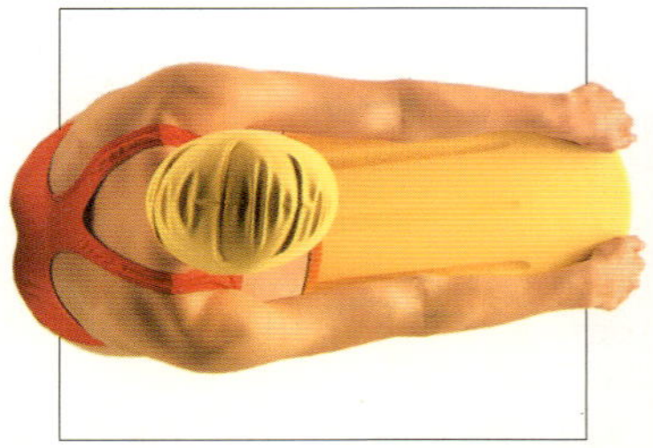

From lying to standing

From your front

When you first glide on your front without a kickboard, you might find it difficult to stand up afterward. Try to think of the following points as you are about to leave your glide position.

Exercising Try this first when you are close to the pool wall.

1 Raise your head and press downward and backward with your hands at the same time. Your legs will then start to sink.

2 As your legs start to sink, bend your knees and bring them up toward your chest.

Plant your feet firmly on the bottom.

3 As your body rotates, your feet will begin to point downward. Lower your legs and stand up.

From your back

Traveling backward is less natural than traveling forward, so you will find that standing up after gliding on your back is an important skill to learn.

1 Drop your chin onto your chest and circle your hands backward until they are level with your shoulders and close to the surface.

2 As your legs sink, bend your knees into your chest and scoop your hands toward your feet.

3 As you rotate, swing your knees under you and point your feet downward. Lower your feet and stand up.

Push and glide on your back

Practicing push and glide on your back will help you improve your backstroke start or turn.

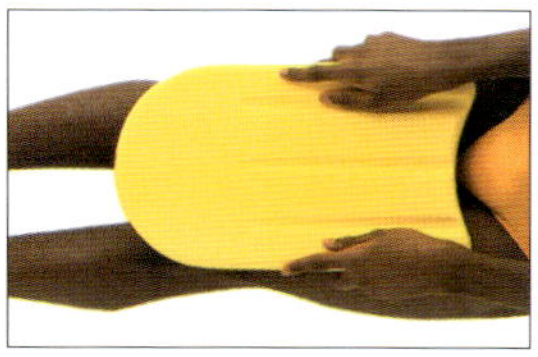

Holding one kickboard

Try this exercise with just one kickboard, too. Hold the sides of the kickboard and lay it flat along your thighs at arms length.

Standing up If you want to stand up, it is easier if you let go of the kickboard and scoop your arms and hands as shown above.

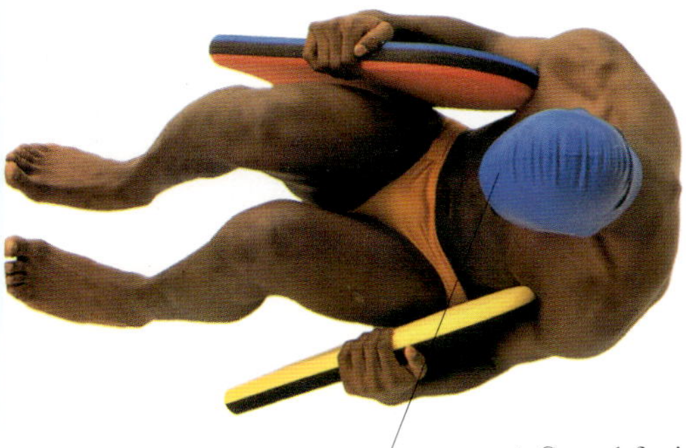

Keep your chin tucked in.

1 Stand facing the wall, holding a kickboard under each arm. Bounce gently as you lean back to plant both feet firmly against the wall, just under the surface.

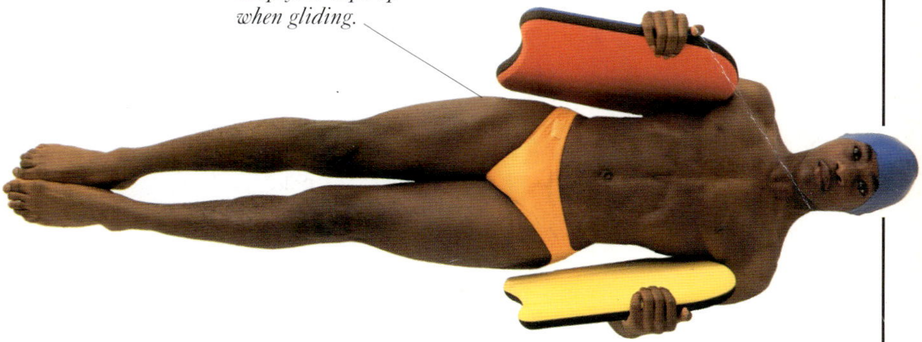

Keep your hips up when gliding.

2 Push off strongly and straighten out both legs, stretching your body out. Try to keep the back of your head just resting in the water, with your ears at surface level.

Early skills

HAVING GAINED confidence in the water, you can try some more advanced activities. One of the most important swimming skills you can learn is sculling. All swimming strokes make use of sculling actions in some way. Just by changing the angle of your wrist you can travel head first, feet first, or even stay in one place. Sculling is also needed to perform other skills, such as treading water or somersaulting.

Stationary sculling

Sculling is a continuous action. Lie on your back and stretch out your hands, keeping your fingers together. Angle your palms out and down and, leading with your little finger, trace a figure eight with your hands.

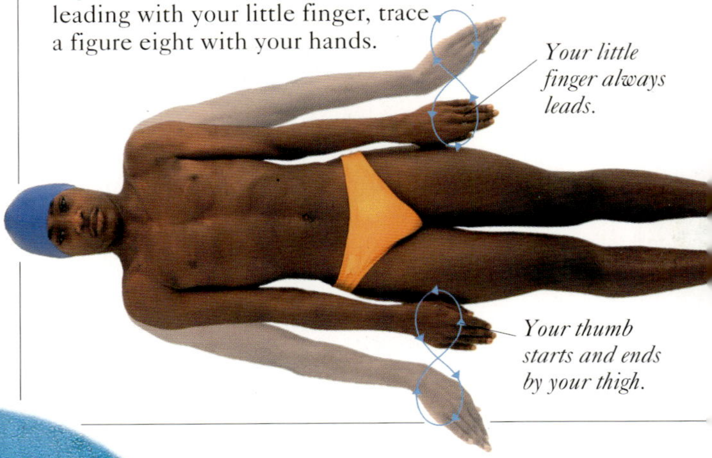

Somersaults

Somersaults in the water help you practice getting your bearings when upside down as well as being fun! Knowing how to do somersaults will also help you when you start to do racing turns.

Forward somersault

When performing a forward somersault, it is easier to begin from a horizontal position on your front.

1 From your front, kick vigorously down with both legs together in a dolphin kick. At the same time, drop your chin onto your chest.

2 Begin to bend your knees and bring them forward toward your chest.

3 As your knees come forward, bend your arms and, turning your hands palms-up, push upward. This will start you rotating into your somersault.

Tuck your knees in tightly.

4 While you are upside-down and still rotating, turn your palms to push toward your feet. This will help you to continue turning.

5 Remain in a curled-up position as you are turning. Your palms should continue to push toward your feet.

6 Continue pushing with your hands. As your head comes around to the surface, open out onto your front again.

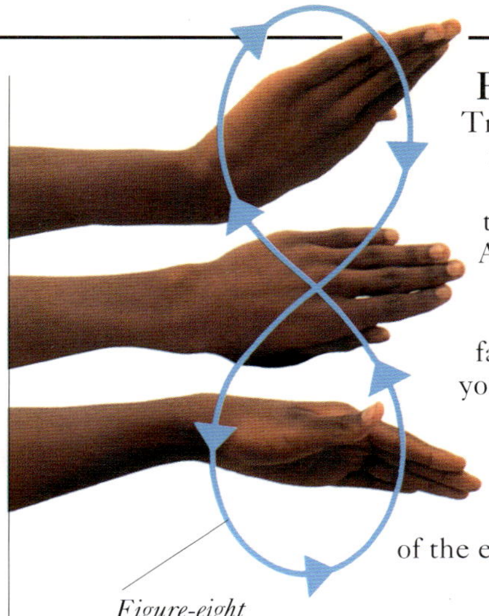

Figure eight

Trace a figure eight, moving your hand away from, then toward, your body. As your hand nears your thigh, your thumb should be facing up, although your little finger still leads. Now rotate your hand so that it travels around the bottom curve of the eight to start again.

Treading water

You will need to know how to tread water if you stop to rest in deep water, or if you need to gather your bearings in open water. Hold your arms out in front of you and scull with your hands, sweeping outward and inward.

Backward somersault

To prevent water from going up your nose as you somersault backward, slowly bubble air through your nose while you somersault. Alternatively, you can wear a nose clip.

1 From lying in the water on your back, drop your head backward into the water, bend your knees, and begin to press your hands downward and backward.

2 To continue to rotate backward, push down with your hands. Your feet will pass over your head.

3 As you rotate, you will pass through a sitting position under the water. Press down with your palms and lift your hips toward the surface.

4 Continue pressing down with your palms and lift your knees toward the surface.

5 Scoop your hands down and back and continue to lift your knees.

6 Look for the surface, then begin to open out onto your back again.

On the move

TRY OUT SOME of the water confidence exercises shown here before you learn the main swimming strokes. Activities such as opening your eyes underwater, blowing bubbles, and breathing in and out as you lift your head in and out of the water will help you to become more familiar with the feel of the water.

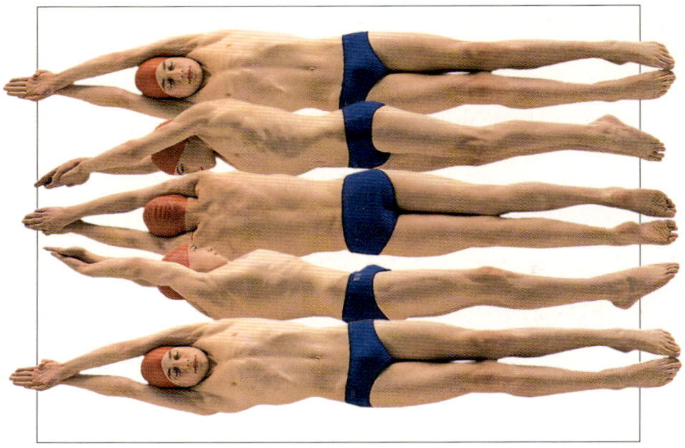

Rolling
This simple rolling exercise will make you aware of a new way to move in the water. Take up a gliding position, with back stretched. Now, by using only the muscles in your back and abdomen, roll over onto your side, then onto your front, and finally return to your back.

Log roll
This exercise is sometimes called a log roll. Try to do one quickly without stopping. Can you turn in the opposite direction too?

Surface dive

One way of submerging efficiently is to use a headfirst surface dive. The advantage of this dive is that the first arm action can be part of a swimming stroke, usually breaststroke. You should not wear goggles when doing this dive.

1 From a swimming position, pull down with your hands and begin to bend at your hips. Breathe in just before you lower your head and pull down.

Keep your legs straight along the surface.

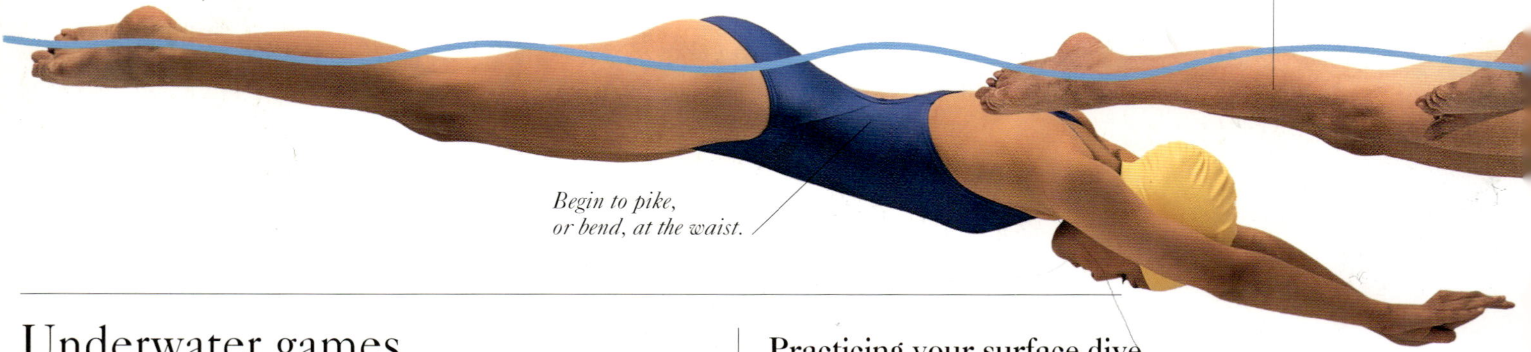

Begin to pike, or bend, at the waist.

Underwater games

To familiarize yourself with both breathing and seeing underwater, try these games with friends in the shallow part of the pool, away from any diving.

Swimming through legs
Take turns swimming through your friends' legs. Try to avoid coming into contact with their legs.

Making faces
Practice opening your eyes underwater by seeing who can make the silliest face.

Practicing your surface dive
Diving for rings on the bottom of the pool is a good way to practice your surface dive. You could even form teams with other swimmers and have a relay competition.

Do not challenge others on how long you can stay underwater.

Traveling through the water

How you move through the water depends on how you use your arms and hands, and legs and feet. An important rule to remember is that for every action, there is an equal and opposite reaction. If you push back, you will move forward; if you push down, you will lift up.

Front paddle

Knowing how to swim front, or "doggie," paddle will help you when you get to the crawl. It is an easy stroke since your hands stay under the water and you can swim with your head above the water, but it is more efficient to keep your head lowered.

2 Bend at the hips and sweep your arms toward your legs until they are parallel. Then turn your hands so that your palms press down toward the pool bottom.

3 As you press down with your hands, raise your legs, keeping them together and straight.

4 When your legs are pointing straight up, your hands should be pointing to the floor of the pool. The weight of your legs above the surface will start to drive you downward.

Back paddle

Back paddle is one way of traveling on your back. Push off on your back from a wall, and make small movements from your wrists and elbows with both hands.

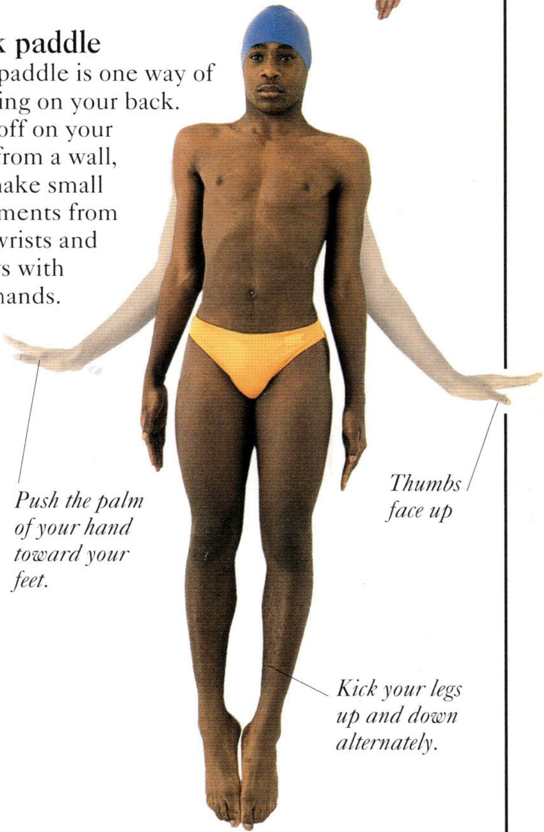

Breathing exercise

If you can't breathe comfortably when swimming, your speed and the distances you can cover will be limited. The two main breathing methods are explosive and trickle; you either blow the air out quickly or let it trickle out slowly. Practice each method while standing in shallow water to decide which is best for you.

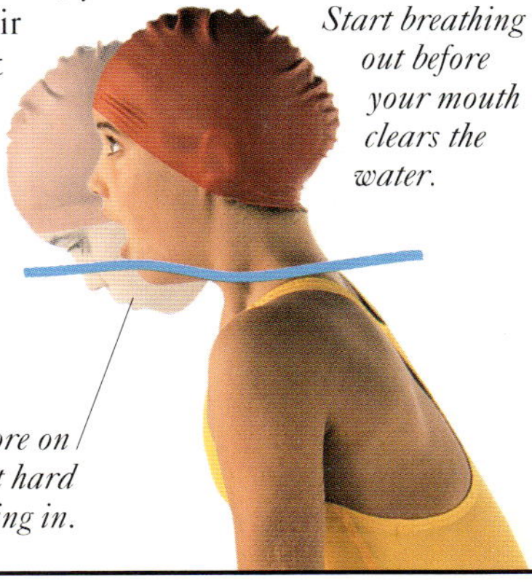

The crawl

THE CRAWL IS the fastest and most efficient of all the swimming strokes. To swim it correctly, your body must be streamlined and horizontal, and your legs and arms must move continuously. Each arm, in turn, propels you through the water. At the same time, your legs kick up and down to keep you balanced. Your face stays in the water, even when you turn to breathe. In competition, there is no actual event called the crawl, but it is the most common choice of stroke in the freestyle event.

Arm position

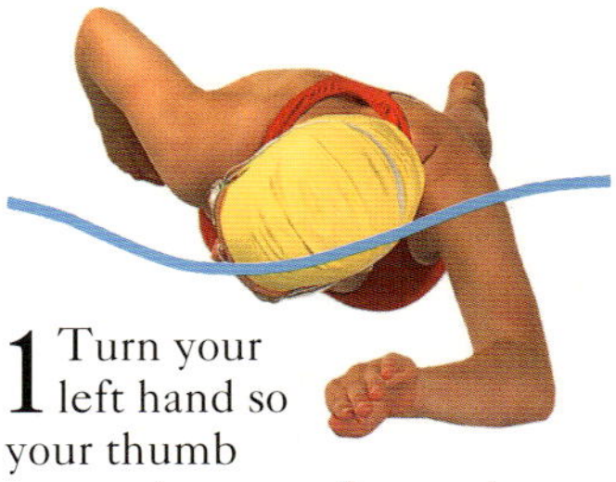

1 Turn your left hand so your thumb enters the water first, palm angled out and down. Your arm should be bent slightly and close to your body's center line. Turn rather than lift your head to breathe.

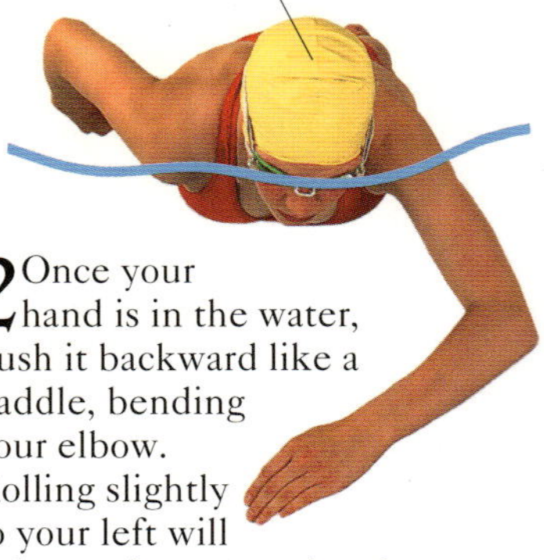

2 Once your hand is in the water, push it backward like a paddle, bending your elbow. Rolling slightly to your left will help you keep your hand close to the center line.

How to breathe out

You can either use "trickle" breathing, gradually letting the air out while your face is still in the water, as shown here, or "explosive" breathing, when you blow the air out very hard just as you turn your head out of the water to breathe in.

When to breathe in

Michelle Smith, the Irish Olympic gold medalist, turns her head toward the arm leaving the water. She opens her mouth wide and takes a deep breath in behind the bow wave before turning her head back to face downward.

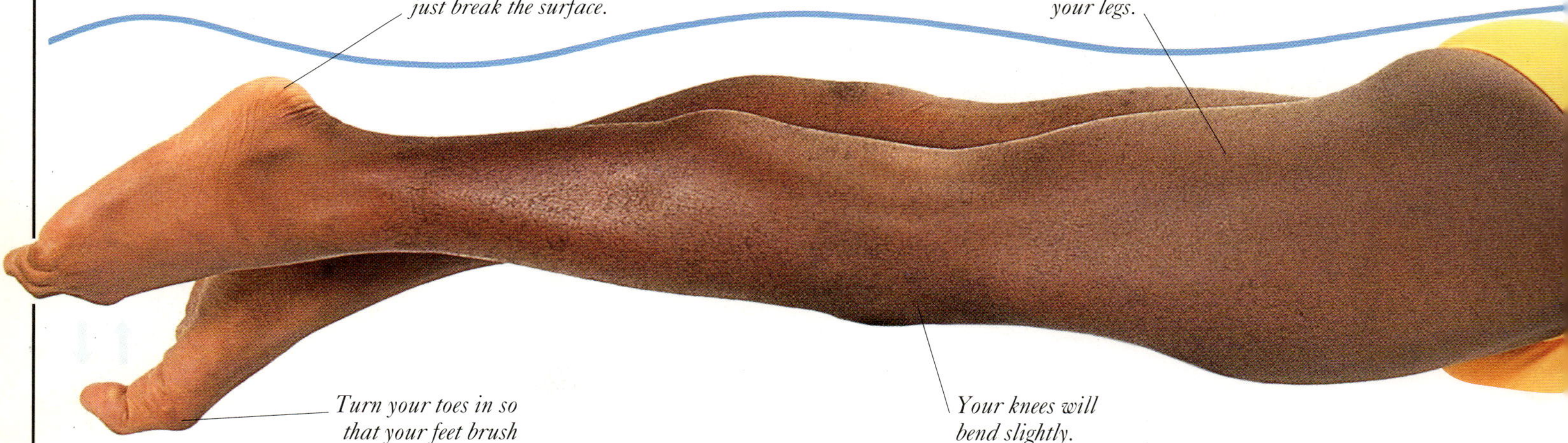

Coordination

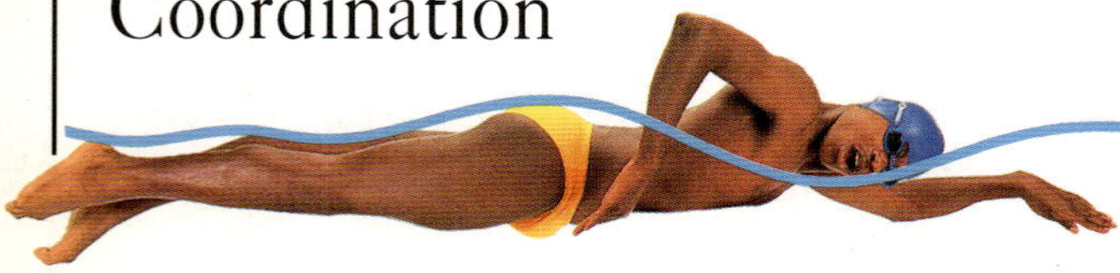

1 As you stretch your left arm out in front of you, turn your head to the right, take a quick breath in, then turn your face back into the water. As your right hand exits, by your thigh, your body should roll to your left.

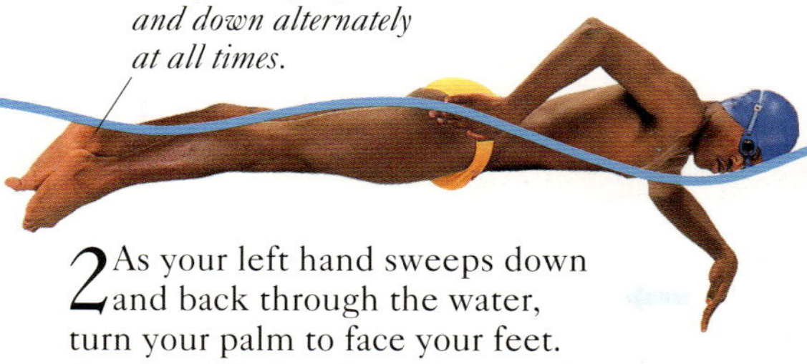

2 As your left hand sweeps down and back through the water, turn your palm to face your feet. As your right hand travels over the water your upper arm should pass close to your ear.

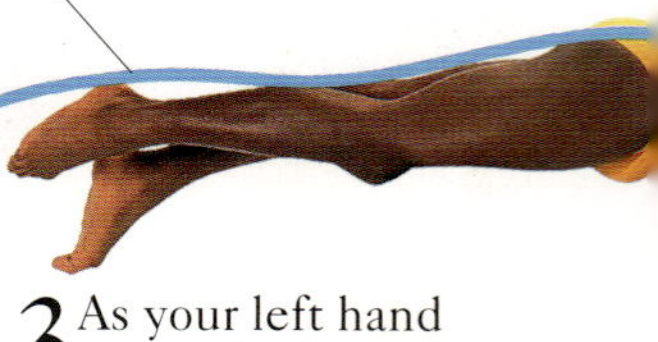

3 As your left hand moves back toward your thigh, reach your right hand forward ready for entry.

Alternate arms
Your right arm alternates with your left arm in exactly the same way.

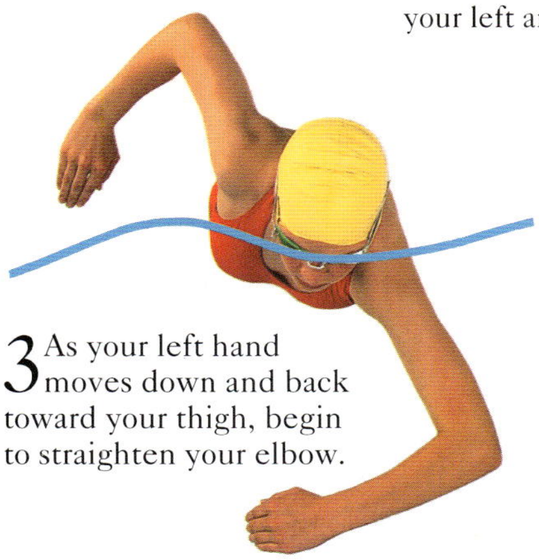

3 As your left hand moves down and back toward your thigh, begin to straighten your elbow.

Keep looking forward and down.

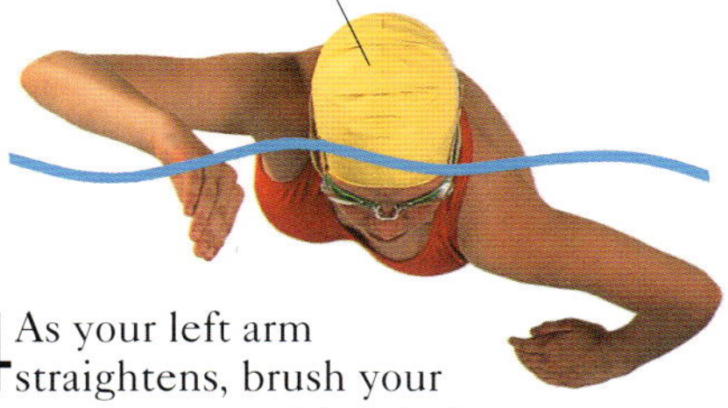

4 As your left arm straightens, brush your thumb past your thigh. Lift your left elbow so that it leaves the water first, before your hand. Turn your hand so that your little finger leads.

Warming up
To increase the flexibility of your shoulders and spine, try this exercise. Place one hand over the back of the other, stretch your arms above your head, then gently bend from side to side, keeping your body straight.

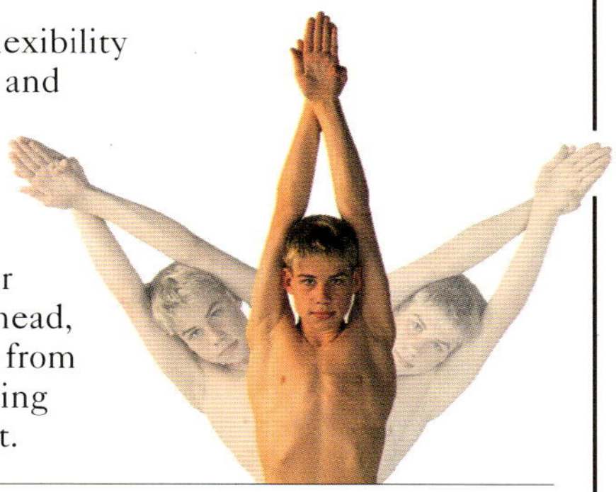

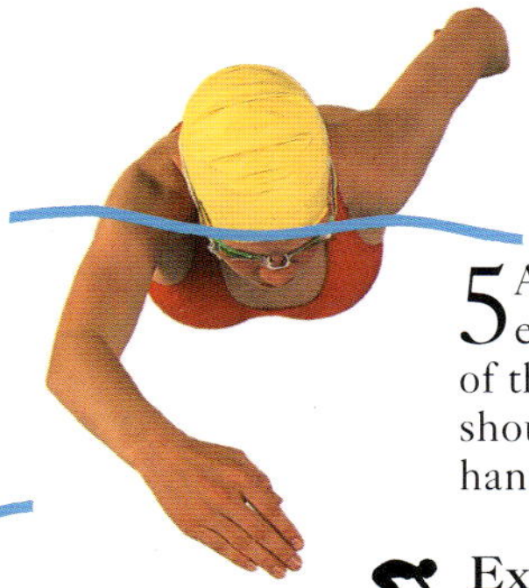

5 As you raise your left elbow and hand clear of the water, roll your shoulders toward the hand entering the water.

Leg strengthening
For this exercise, kick hard, up and down, starting the movement from your hips and finishing it with a whiplike action at your stretched ankles and feet.

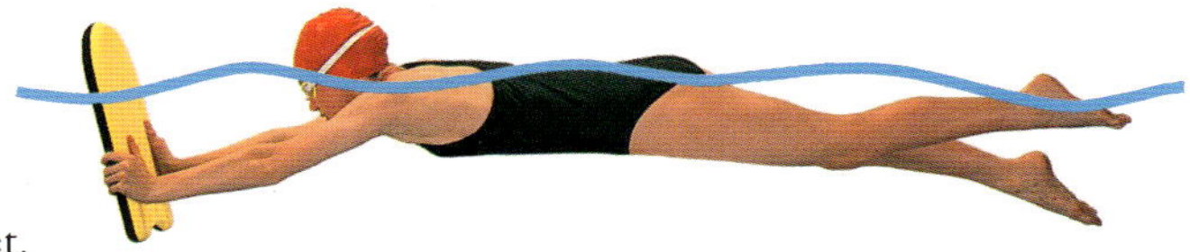

Exercising
Always ask for your coach's advice before doing any exercises.

Streamlined body
Imagine a straight line running down the center of your body, from your forehead to your feet. Try to keep your hands and feet as close as possible to this imaginary line at all times. Rolling your body toward the hand leaving the water will help. Turn your head just enough to allow you to breathe.

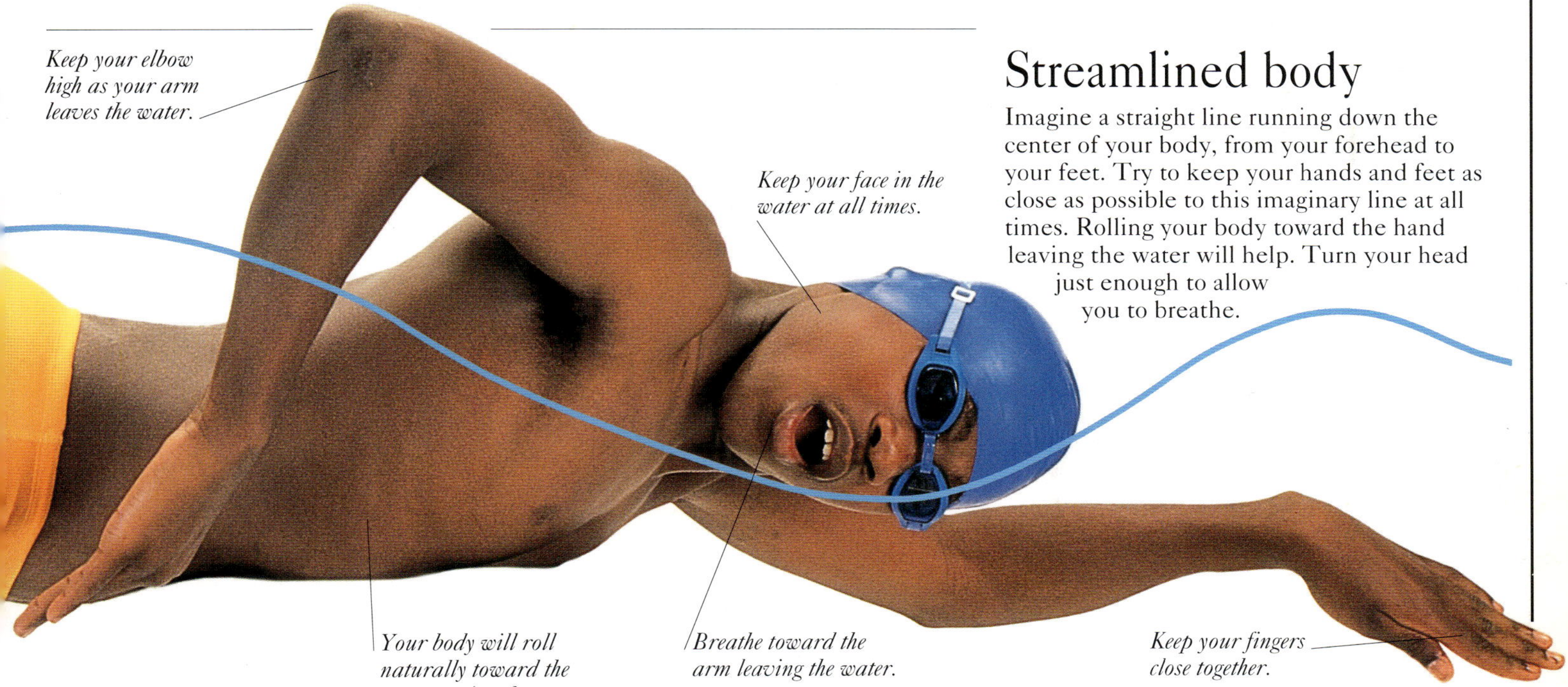

Keep your elbow high as your arm leaves the water.

Keep your face in the water at all times.

Your body will roll naturally toward the arm entering the water.

Breathe toward the arm leaving the water.

Keep your fingers close together.

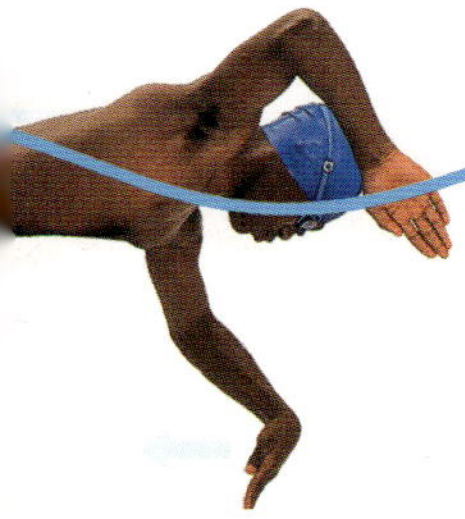

Bend your elbow as you lift your arm.

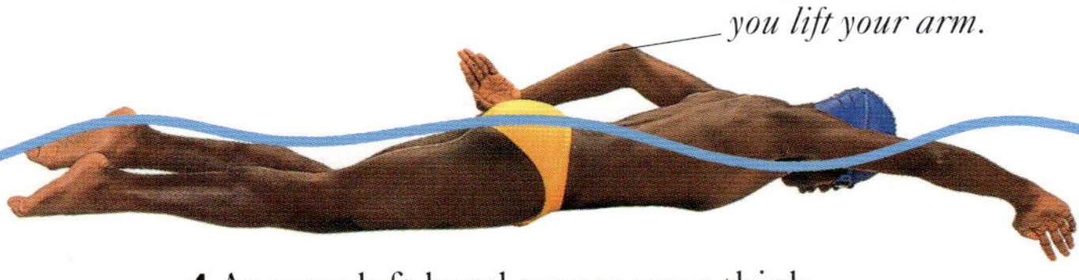

4 As your left hand passes your thigh, it should be turned so that your little finger leads. Lift your left elbow so it leaves the water first, followed by your hand. Your right hand enters the water and starts to pull your body along.

Keep your shoulders level with your head.

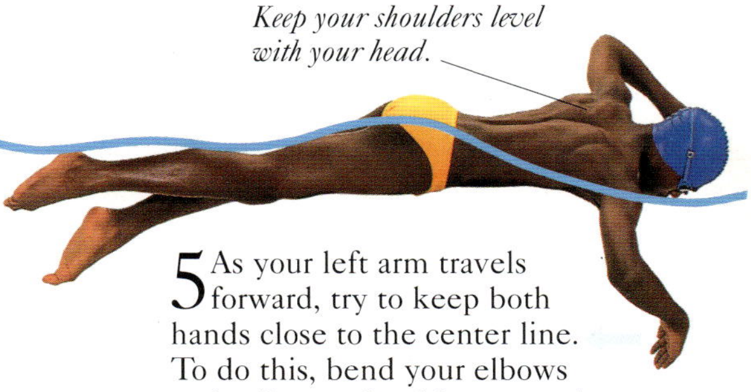

5 As your left arm travels forward, try to keep both hands close to the center line. To do this, bend your elbows and roll your shoulders toward the hand entering the water.

Backstroke

Backstroke is not as fast as the crawl or butterfly, but it is still the fastest method of traveling on your back. You should aim for a streamlined body position, while inclining your body slightly to keep your kick under the water. Make sure that your arms and legs move continuously at all times.

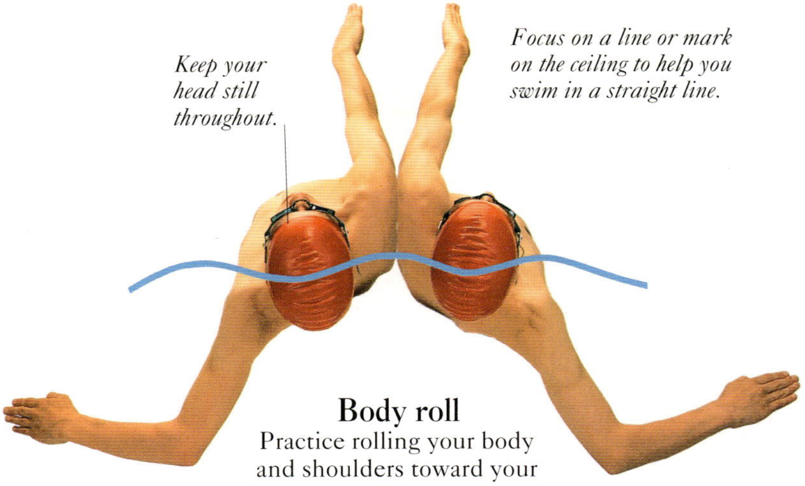

Body roll
Practice rolling your body and shoulders toward your entering arm. This will place your entering hand into a better position for propulsion and your exiting hand into a better position for recovery.

Streamlined
Here you can see Jeff Rouse swimming in the backstroke event at Phoenix, AZ, 1996.

"My hips and body are rotating toward my arm that is about to enter the water. This rotation helps me keep my body in the most streamlined position possible."

Alternate arms
Your arms should work continuously, your right arm alternating with your left.

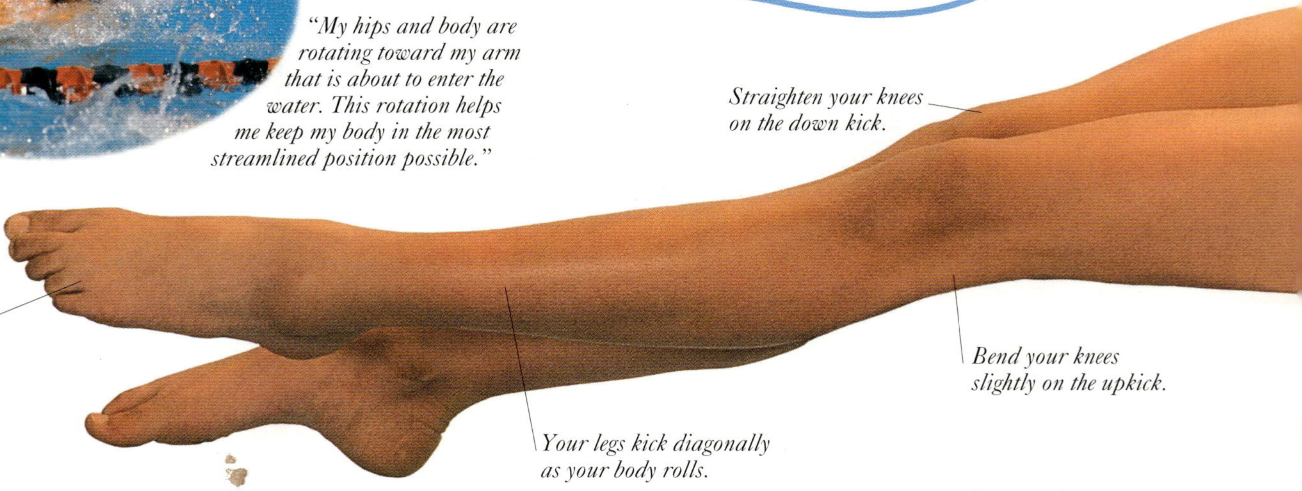

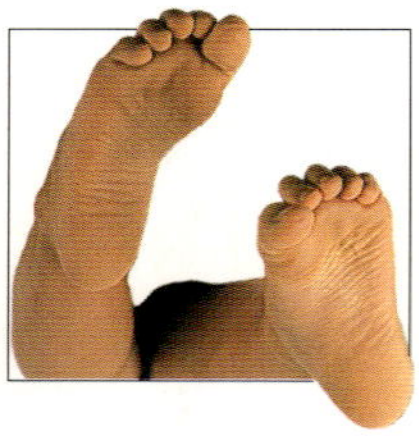

Intoeing
Your feet will make more efficient paddles if you turn them inward, so that your big toes brush past each other.

Breathing
Practice breathing in as one arm recovers and out as the other arm recovers.

Coordination

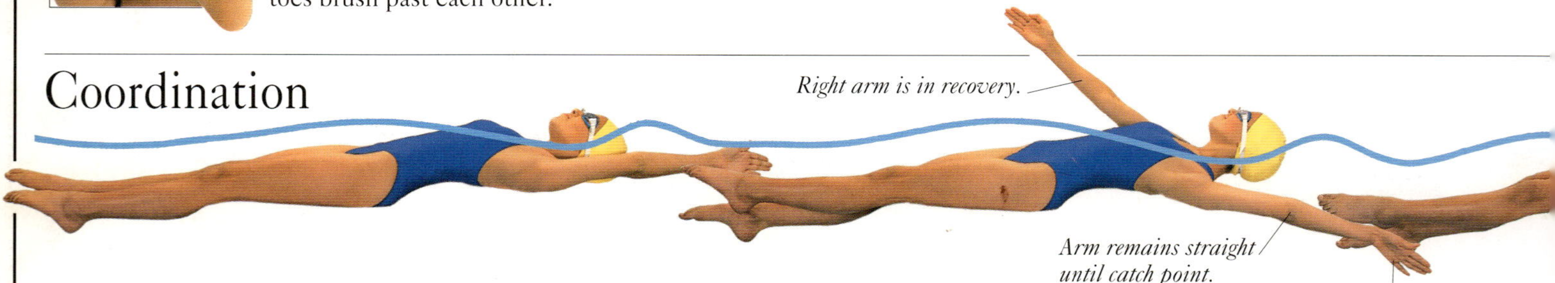

1 This sequence explains the efficient bent arm, or "S" pull. Keep your left arm in line with your shoulder as your left hand enters the water. Your little finger leads, palm facing out and arm fully stretched. Your right arm should be about to exit.

2 Once your left hand is in the water, turn your palm to face down and stretch your hand forward, down, and out to catch point, 6-8 in (15-20 cm) below the surface. Roll your body toward your left arm as your right arm begins its recovery over the water.

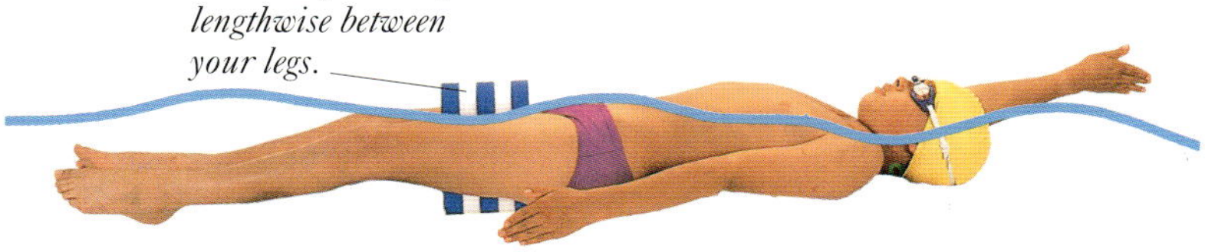

Arms-only exercise
Use a pull buoy to keep your hips and legs close to the surface, while you practice arms-only swimming to strengthen your arms and improve your stroke.

In recovery
Here, Great Britain's Susan Rolph demonstrates a classic recovery position. As her stretched arm sweeps back, it brushes by her ear, close to her body's central line.

Body position
Your body should be nearly horizontal, with the back of your head in a natural line with your spine and your ears just level with the water surface. Your feet should be slightly lower than your head. Your arms will alternate between propulsion and recovery, with your body rolling toward the propulsive arm each time. Your legs kick alternately throughout.

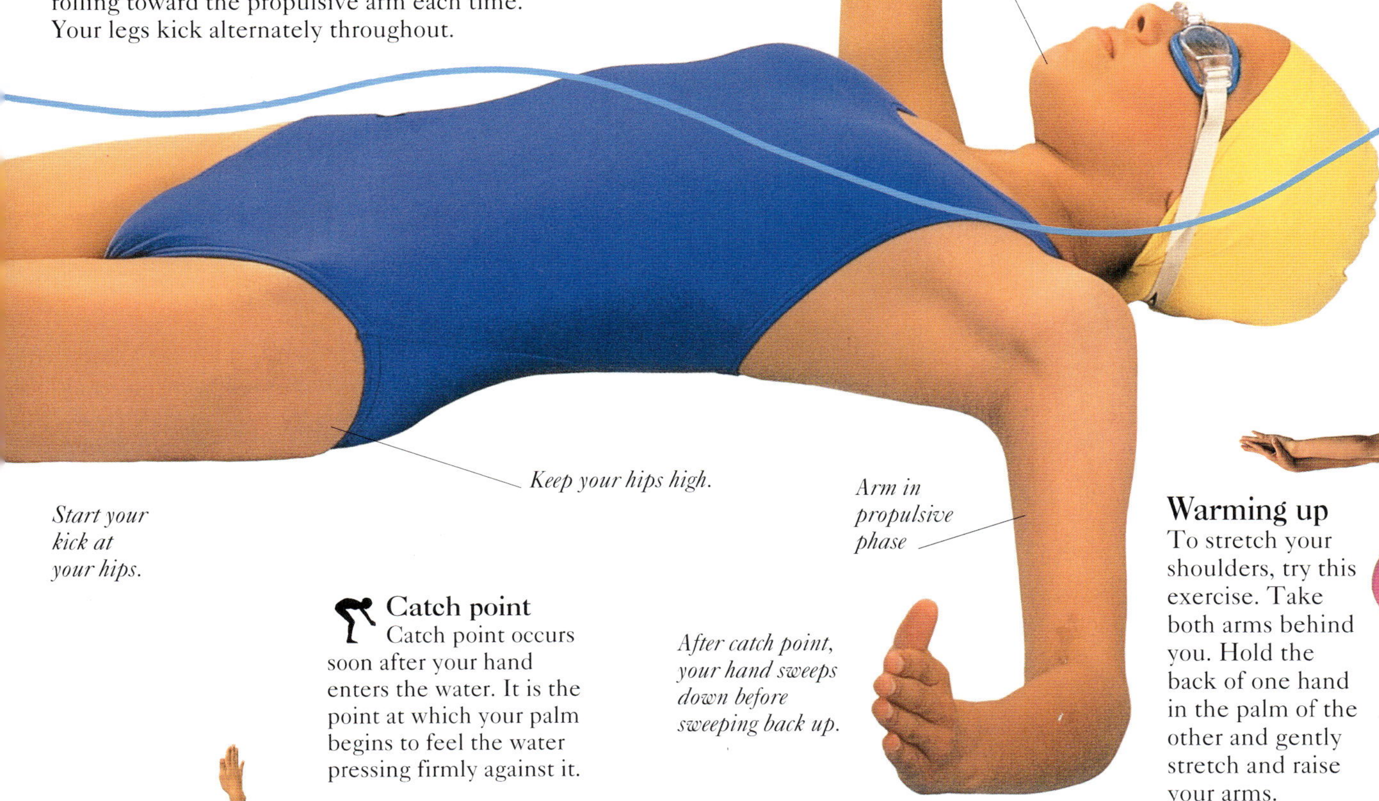

Catch point
Catch point occurs soon after your hand enters the water. It is the point at which your palm begins to feel the water pressing firmly against it.

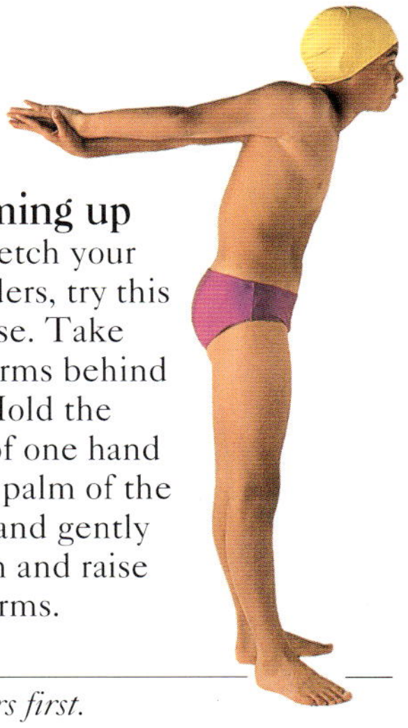

Warming up
To stretch your shoulders, try this exercise. Take both arms behind you. Hold the back of one hand in the palm of the other and gently stretch and raise your arms.

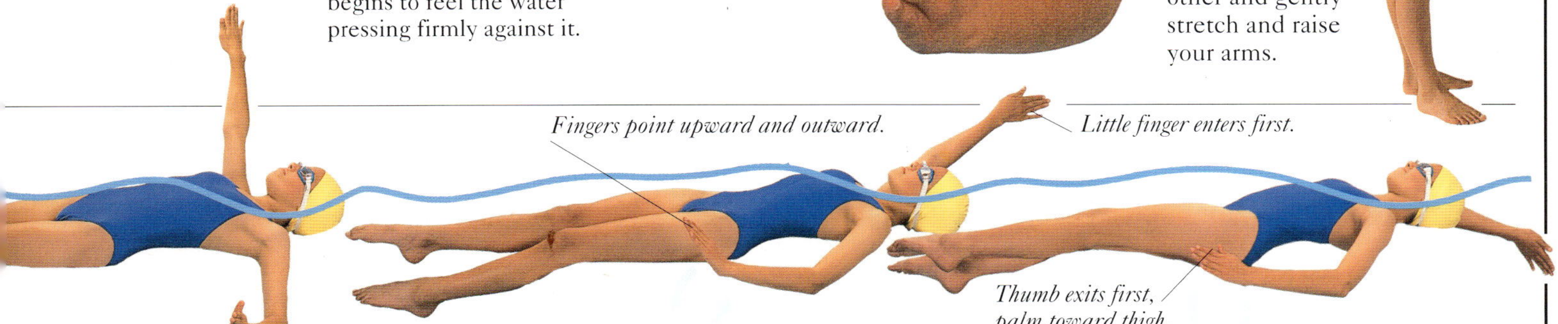

3 After catch point, your elbow bends as your left hand pushes down and back, until it is in line with your shoulder. Continue to roll to the left.

4 Your elbow will pass through an angle of about 90° as you sweep your left hand toward your feet and up. When your left hand is just below the surface, your right hand will be ready to enter the water.

5 Sweep your left hand down vigorously and then back up, bringing your hand close to your thigh. Then straighten your left arm as it leaves the water, and begin to roll your body to your right.

Breaststroke

Exercising
Try to spread your knees just wider than hip width as you drive your legs around and back. This way, your legs will recover faster and will be ready to give you more propulsion sooner.

IN BREASTSTROKE, your arms and legs stay under the surface all the time. This means you have more water resistance to overcome and it is the main reason why breaststroke is the slowest of the four strokes. It is an easy, enjoyable stroke to learn since you can raise your head above the surface to breathe. Practice the leg kick while holding a kickboard, before adding the arm actions.

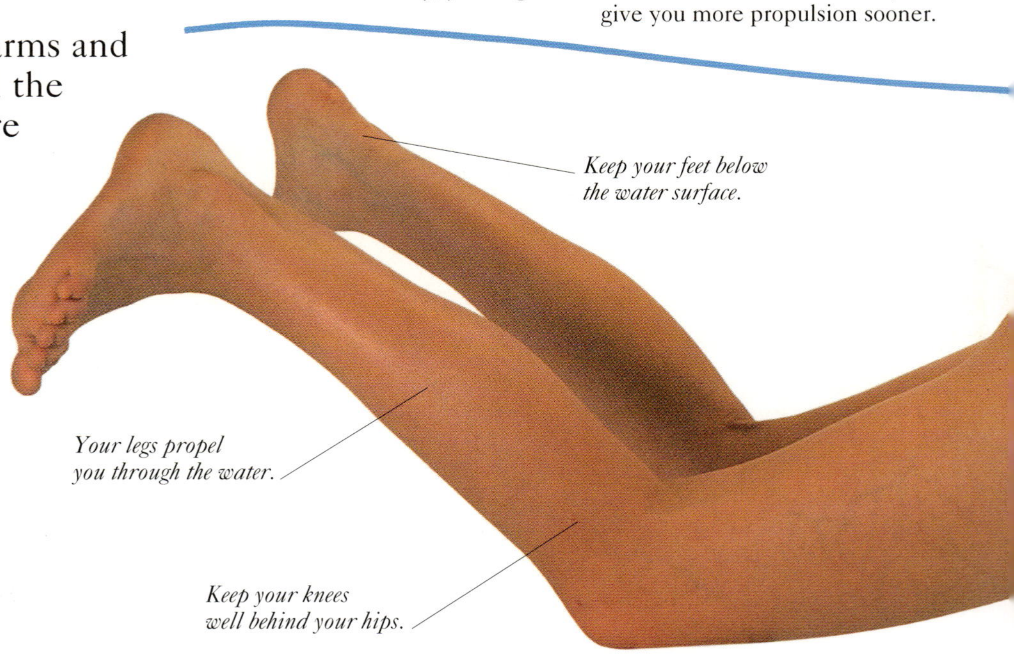

Coordination

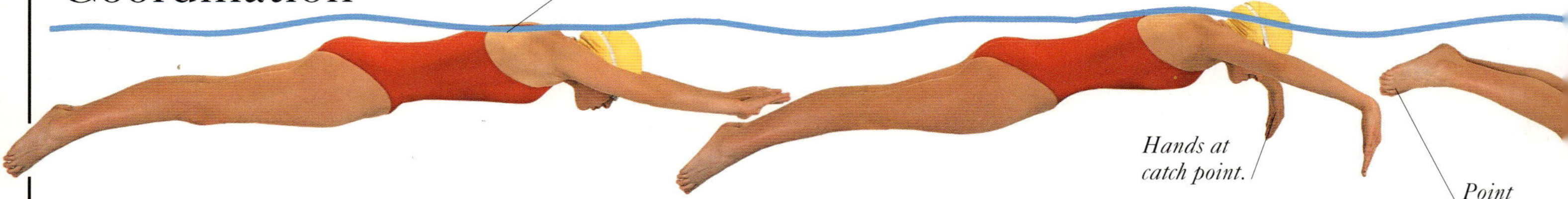

1 Start from a good, fully stretched push-and-glide position with your ears squeezed between your arms. Try and get into this position between each full stroke. Your coach might advise you to reduce this glide as your swimming improves.

2 From the glide, sweep your hands outward to a point just wider than shoulder width, then turn your palms down. This point is known as catch point. The rest of your body remains in the same position as before.

Breaststroke competition
Here, swimmers can be seen using the "high-lift" style in the women's breaststroke event at the International Swimming Cup in 1990. Nowadays, many swimmers use this style to improve their speed.

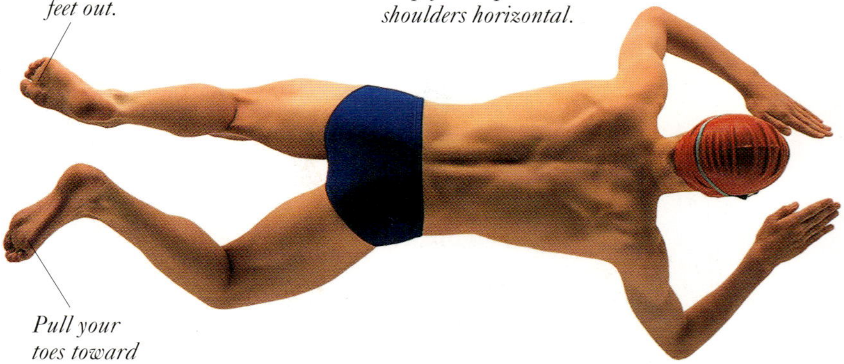

The whip kick
The whip kick helps you get the most out of the powerful thrust of your legs. After bringing your heels up close to your buttocks, with your knees about hip-width apart, turn your feet up and out and kick vigorously around and back.

Body position

To swim breaststroke well, angle your body from your shoulders, so your feet stay under the surface. As you push your legs back and around, your arms should be stretching forward, with your head almost under the surface.

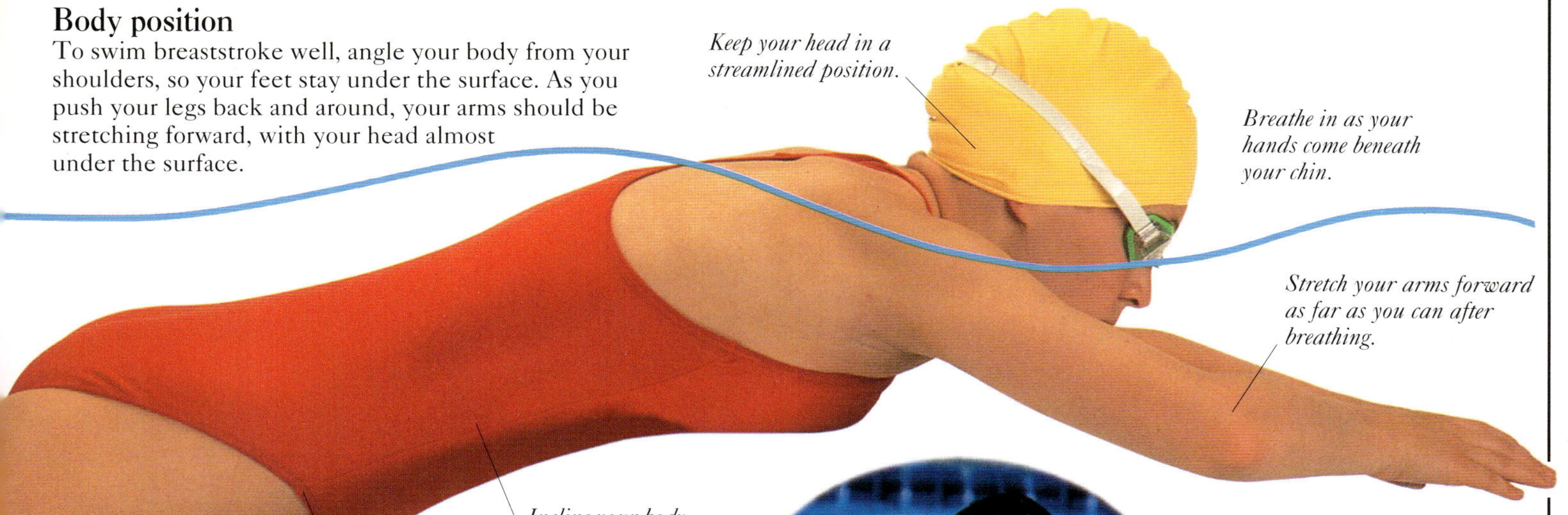

The high-lift style

Here, Krisztina Egerszegy of Hungary swims breaststroke by lifting her upper body out of the water and moving her hips up and down in a wave-like action. This reduces water resistance, helping her swim faster.

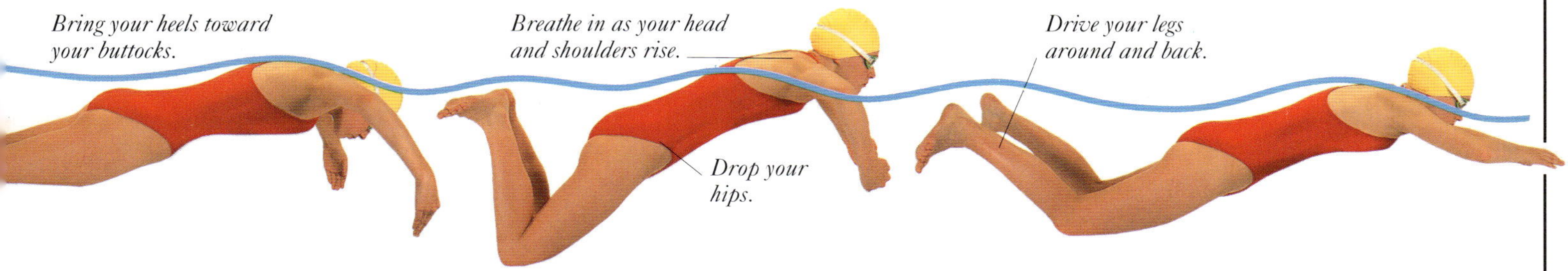

3 After catch point, bend your elbows sharply so that your palms sweep around, down, and back. Gradually start lifting your head and shoulders forward and up and begin to bend your knees.

4 Continue to bend your elbows and circle your hands. After they pass below your elbows, begin to bring them up toward your chin. Turn your feet up and out, ready to drive back.

5 Stretch your arms forward, and return to the original glide position, lowering your head back so you are streamlined once again.

After catch point

Once your hands have reached catch point, they begin the propulsive stage. Press your hands out, down, and back as you begin to bend your arms.

Arm action

In order to improve your propulsion through the water keep your shoulders horizontal and your elbows high. Sweep your hands back and in toward your chest, pushing against the water as you do so.

Thigh and ankle warm-up

Supporting yourself against a wall, hold your foot and slowly and gently pull it back to your thigh.

Butterfly

BUTTERFLY WAS INVENTED in the early 1930s but was swum as a version of breaststroke until 1952, when it was officially recognized as a new stroke. Originally the kick was similar to that used in breaststroke, but now the more efficient up-and-down "dolphin kick" is used. Because your arms recover over the water and your legs and body undulate there is far less resistance and more propulsion than in breaststroke.

Arm position

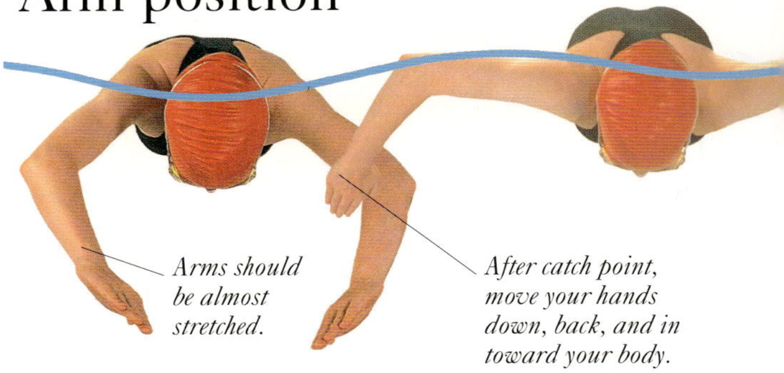

1 Your hands enter the water about shoulder-width apart, thumbs first and palms angled outward. Your face should be in the water.

2 After entry, sweep your hands outward to catch point, just outside your shoulders, then bend your elbows.

Coordination

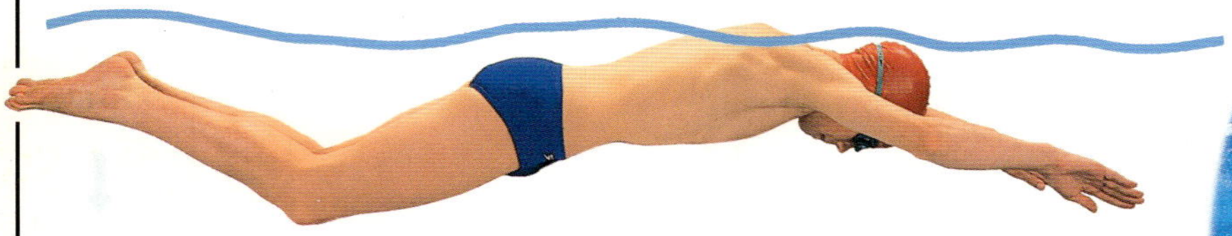

1 As your hands enter the water, kick down, starting your kick from your hips. The downbeat will cause your hips to rise. Keep your ankles and toes stretched.

Butterfly race

Notice the powerful arm recovery of the swimmers in this picture, which shows the men's butterfly event at the International Swimming Cup, Rome, Italy 1990.

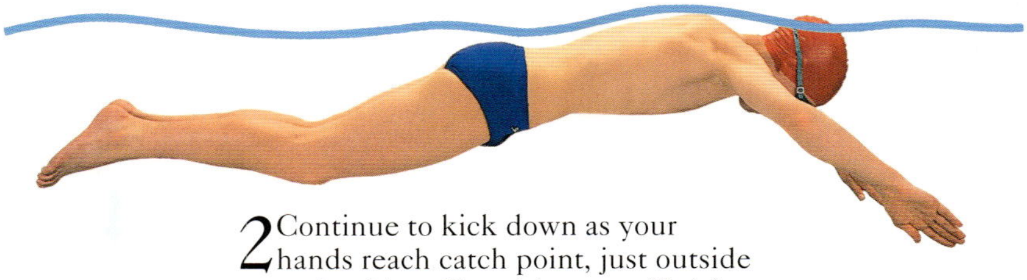

2 Continue to kick down as your hands reach catch point, just outside your shoulders. Your hips are still rising.

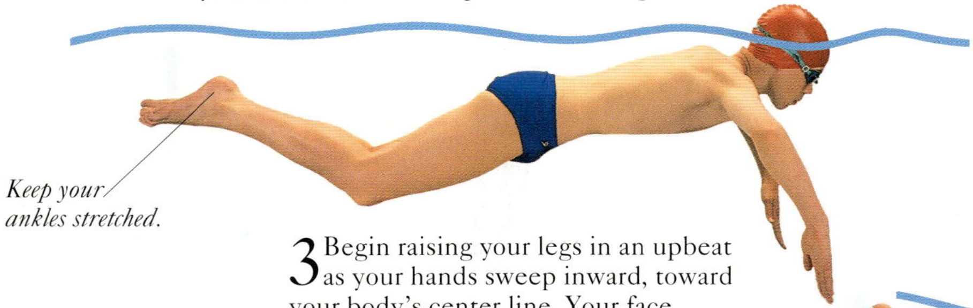

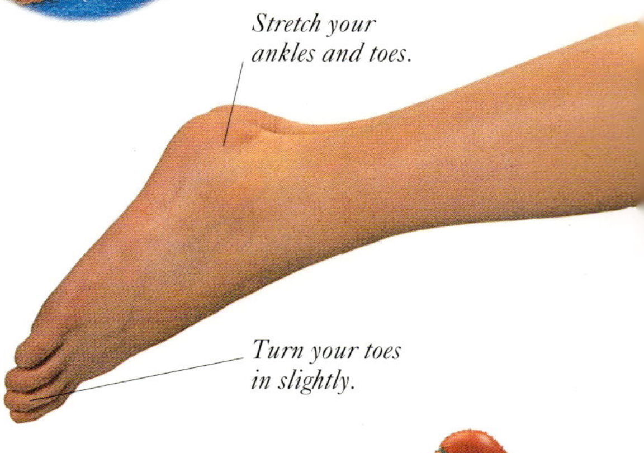

3 Begin raising your legs in an upbeat as your hands sweep inward, toward your body's center line. Your face remains in the water, but your head rises a little. Start to drop your hips.

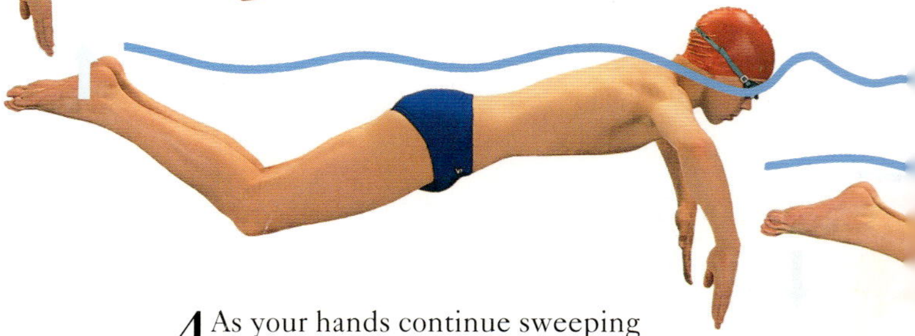

4 As your hands continue sweeping in and back, your legs are still on the upbeat and your head keeps rising. Your hips continue to drop.

Taking a breath

Here, Hayley Lewis of Australia is about to lower her head back into the water after breathing, but before her arms finish their recovery.

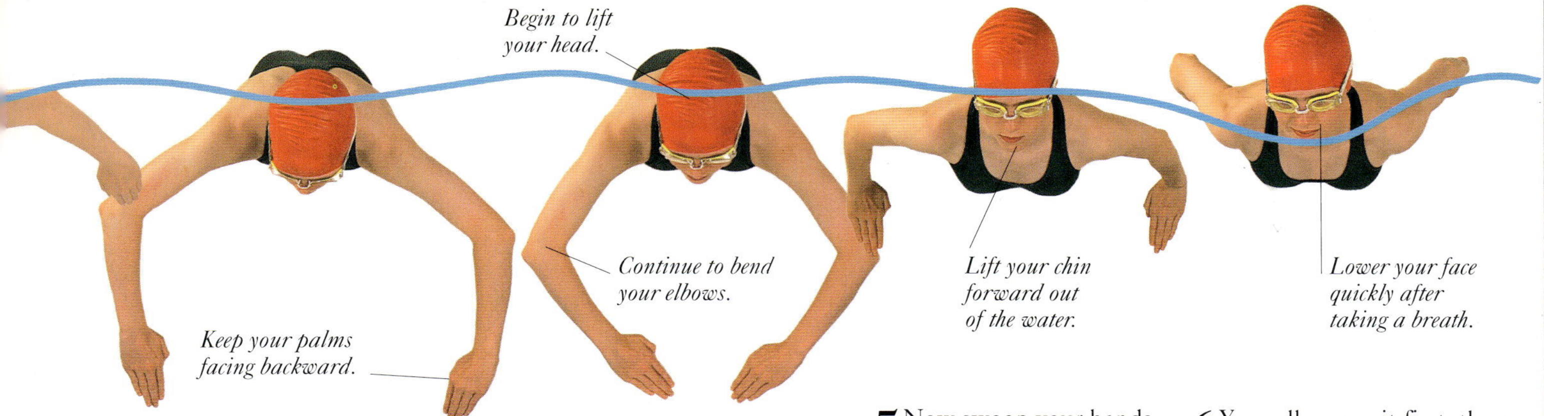

3 Your elbows should continue to bend as your hands sweep in toward the center line. Your face should remain in the water.

4 Your fingers should almost touch as you sweep your hands in and back until they are just beneath your stomach.

5 Now sweep your hands outward, palms still facing backward. They should pass close by your thighs before exiting.

6 Your elbows exit first, then your hands, little fingers first and palms facing in. Snap your face back into the water as your arms swing forward.

Body position

To swim butterfly well, your body should undulate in a wavelike fashion, alternating between a level, streamlined position and a more inclined position, with your hips high and breaking the water's surface. The head rises up above the water at the end of the underwater arm action.

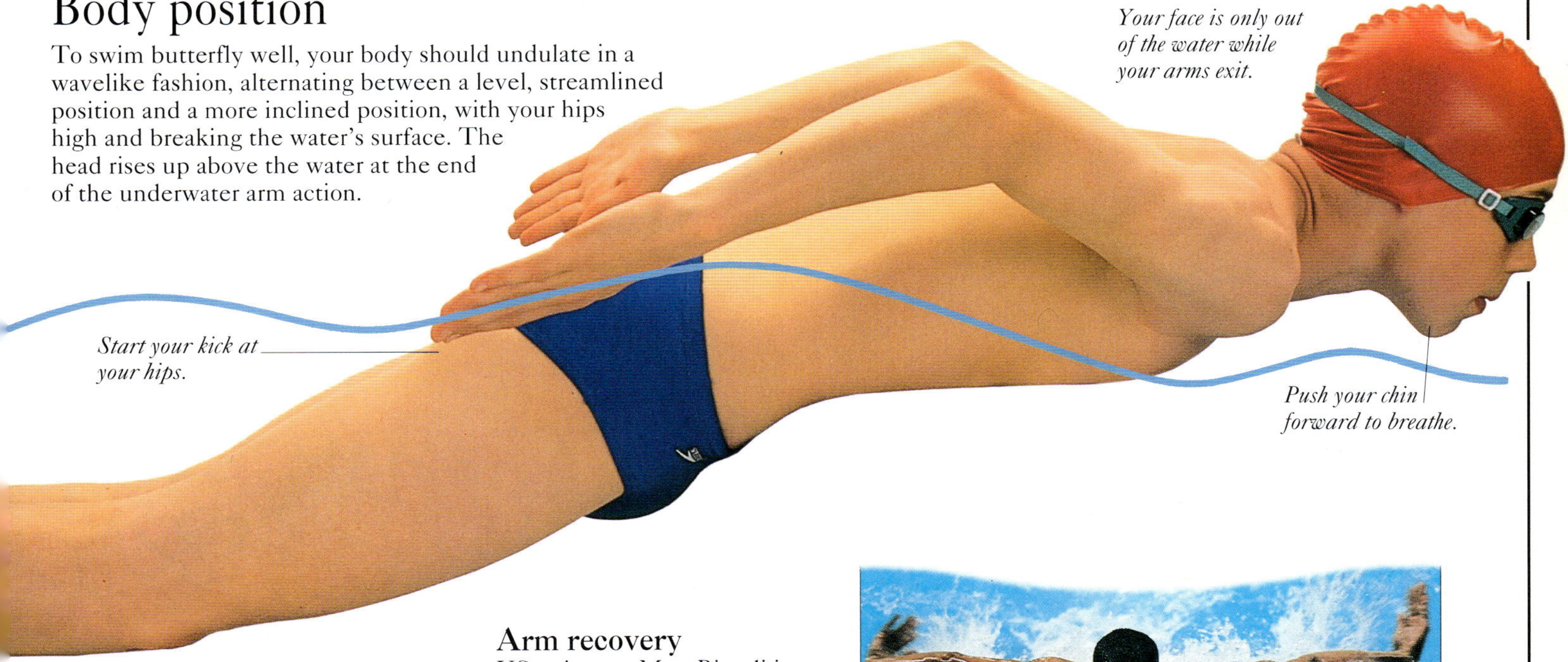

Arm recovery

US swimmer Matt Biondi is one of the world's greatest swimmers. In this picture, you can see how his little fingers remain uppermost as his arms swing around clear of the water during the recovery.

Timing

To remember the two-beat kick, think of kicking once as your arms enter the water and again as they exit.

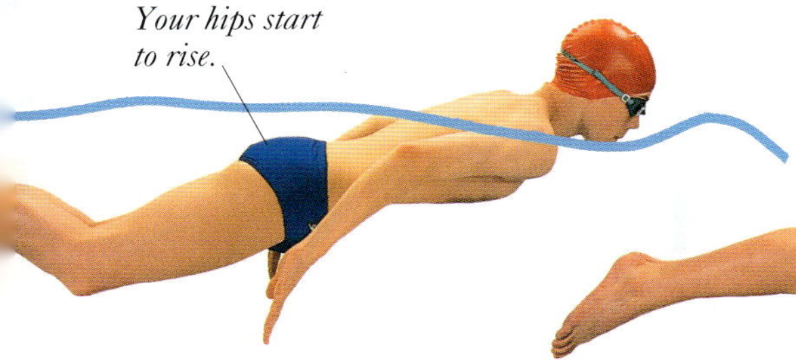

5 As your hands sweep outward past your thighs, ready to exit, your legs start to move back down through the water.

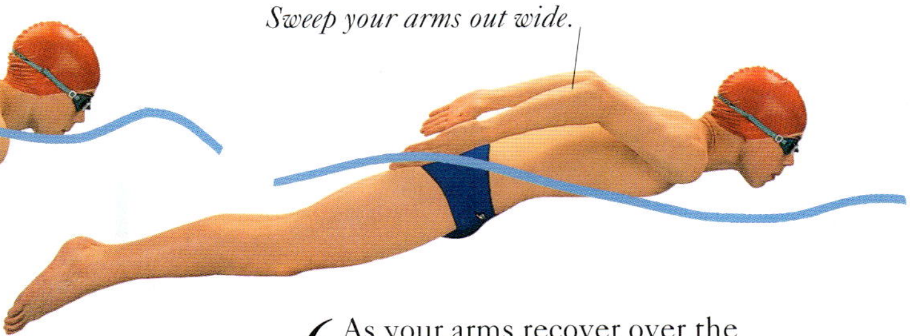

6 As your arms recover over the water, your legs finish their downbeat and start rising again and your hips begin to drop.

Warm-up

This exercise stretches your shoulder and upper arm. Gently pull your elbow across and down your back. Repeat with the other arm.

Racing starts

MAKING A strong start in competitions is vital, especially for swimming short distances. You need to get away from the starting block quickly and accurately judge your flight distance and the angle of entry into the water.

Kneeling dive

A kneeling dive is a good dive to learn first. Position yourself carefully so that you don't slip as you push off. Grip the pool edge with the toes of your front foot. You should travel both up and outward.

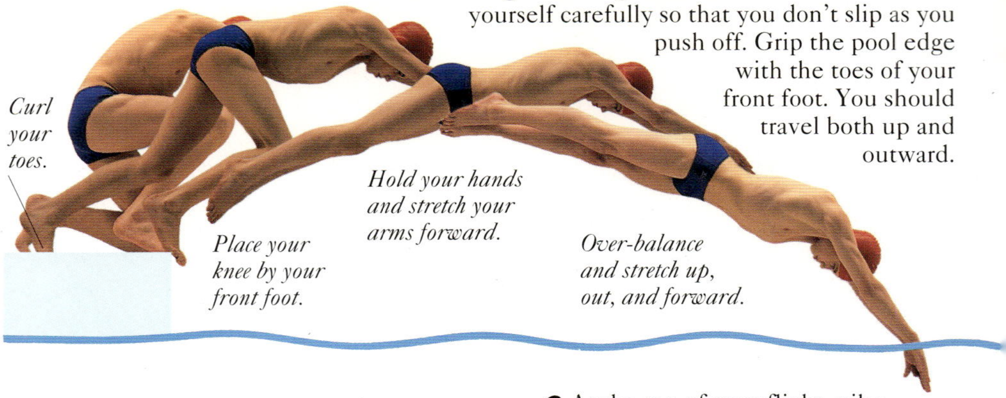

Grab start

The grab start is the most common start for freestyle, breaststroke, and butterfly races, since it helps you get away from the block quickly.

1 At the command "Take your marks," bend down and hold onto the front of the block. Keep your hips above your knees.

2 On the word "Go!" pull sharply on the block. As you over-balance, push off hard with your legs to gain height and distance.

3 At the top of your flight, pike, or bend at the waist. Make sure your head is down as you go into the pike.

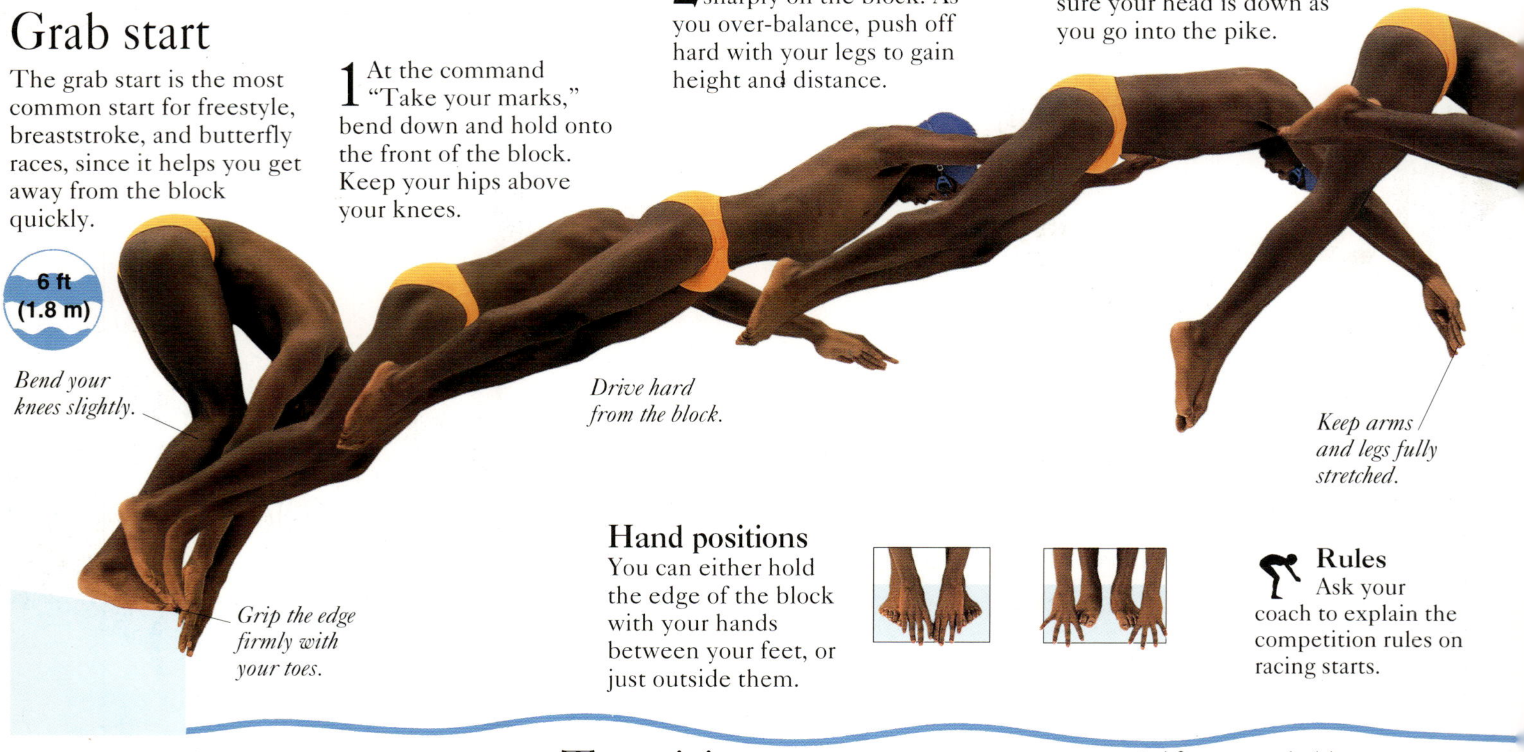

Hand positions

You can either hold the edge of the block with your hands between your feet, or just outside them.

Rules

Ask your coach to explain the competition rules on racing starts.

Other starts

Windup start

Windup starts are used in relay takeovers because you judge your takeoff by the speed of the incoming swimmer. Make a big circular movement up and back with your arms, then drive off powerfully with your legs.

Track start

This start gives a bigger push off. Grip the block with your hands and toes and put your weight on your back foot. Next, pull hard with your arms and push with your feet.

Transition

The crawl

The transition is the time you are underwater between entry and the first arm stroke. Make use of a powerful dive by continuing to stretch.

1 After entry, hold your stretched and streamlined position and flatten out. Then begin to stretch upward in a glide. You will still be traveling at speed.

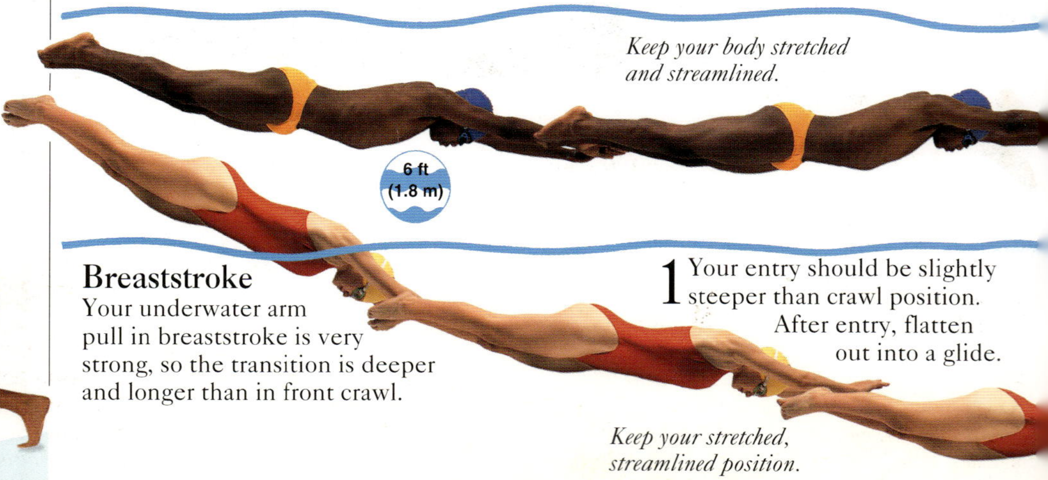

Breaststroke

Your underwater arm pull in breaststroke is very strong, so the transition is deeper and longer than in front crawl.

1 Your entry should be slightly steeper than crawl position. After entry, flatten out into a glide.

Backstroke start

1 Hold the rail and bring your feet up high. Bend your arms and pull your chin to the rail.

2 On the starting signal, throw your head up and back. At the same time, swing your arms up and out and push off hard with your legs.

3 Stretch out, arch your back, and reach toward the water with your fingers. Your fingers should enter the water first.

Backstroke start

The backstroke start begins in the water and is really a backward dive. Face the wall and hold onto the start rail, feet close to the surface. On the word "Go!" push off, stretching up and outward. Do a few kicks underwater before surfacing to start your arm action. For safety, always look behind you before you practice this move.

1996 Olympics

This picture shows the start of a backstroke event. Each swimmer's flight is perfectly streamlined as they reach backward toward entry.

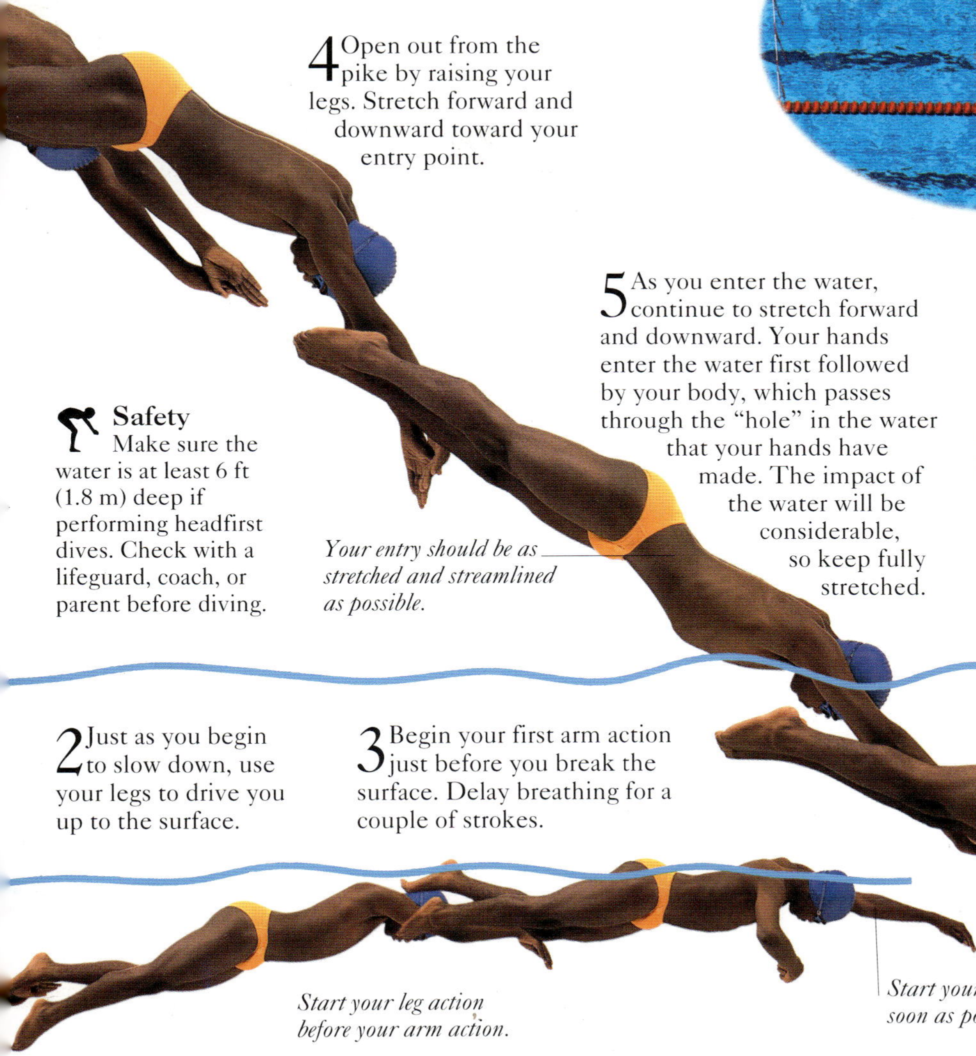

4 Open out from the pike by raising your legs. Stretch forward and downward toward your entry point.

5 As you enter the water, continue to stretch forward and downward. Your hands enter the water first followed by your body, which passes through the "hole" in the water that your hands have made. The impact of the water will be considerable, so keep fully stretched.

Safety

Make sure the water is at least 6 ft (1.8 m) deep if performing headfirst dives. Check with a lifeguard, coach, or parent before diving.

2 Just as you begin to slow down, use your legs to drive you up to the surface.

3 Begin your first arm action just before you break the surface. Delay breathing for a couple of strokes.

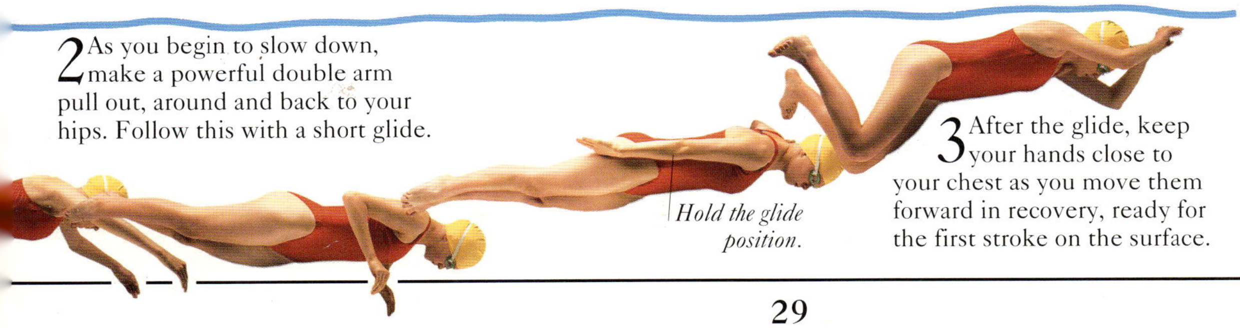

2 As you begin to slow down, make a powerful double arm pull out, around and back to your hips. Follow this with a short glide.

3 After the glide, keep your hands close to your chest as you move them forward in recovery, ready for the first stroke on the surface.

Butterfly transition

This is similar to breaststroke, except it is shorter and shallower. You use a dolphin kick followed by a powerful double arm pull to bring you to the surface.

Racing turns

GOOD TURNS CAN save you valuable time during a race. Make use of your swimming speed as you approach the wall so that you can rotate quickly before planting your feet for a powerful push off. Crawl and backstroke turns include a somersault, while breaststroke and butterfly turns require more of a twisting movement and both your hands and feet touch the wall. Crawl turns are often called "flip" turns, and the breaststroke and butterfly turns are sometimes called "touch" turns. Good turns only come through a lot of practice and hard work.

Backstroke turn

Crawl and backstroke turns are very similar. Use the 16-ft (5-m) warning flags overhead as a guide for when to start your turn.

Crawl turn

To determine the best moment for starting a turn you'll need to experiment with starting at different distances from the wall. To begin with, try starting the somersault at about 3–5 ft (1–1½ m) from the wall, then adjust it according to your results.

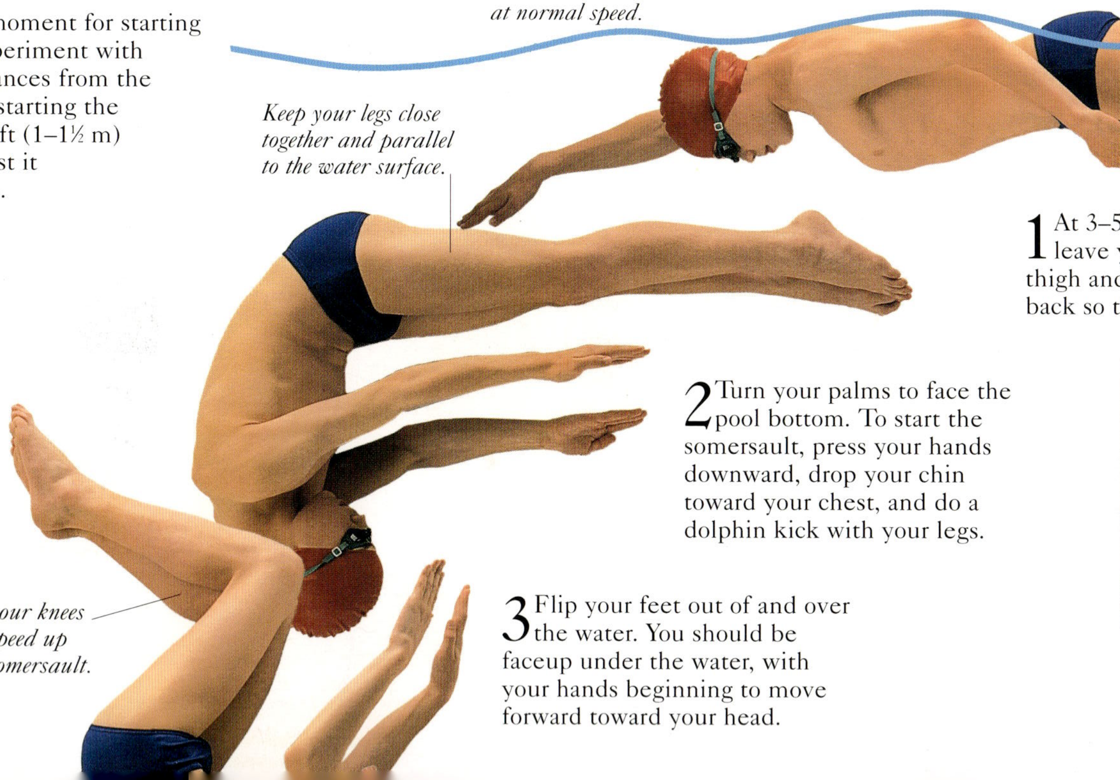

1 At 3–5 ft (1–1½ m) from the wall, leave your trailing hand by your thigh and pull your leading hand back so that it is also by your thigh.

2 Turn your palms to face the pool bottom. To start the somersault, press your hands downward, drop your chin toward your chest, and do a dolphin kick with your legs.

3 Flip your feet out of and over the water. You should be faceup under the water, with your hands beginning to move forward toward your head.

The push off
To get the most out of your turns, practice the push offs on their own, then you can add them to the turn.

Flip turns
It is vital that competition swimmers know how to do fast, efficient turns.

4 Plant your feet against the wall, under the water, then push off as hard as you can, stretching out your arms and pressing them against your ears.

5 As you push off, turn onto your front. Glide, making the most of your push-off speed, then kick your legs and aim for the surface.

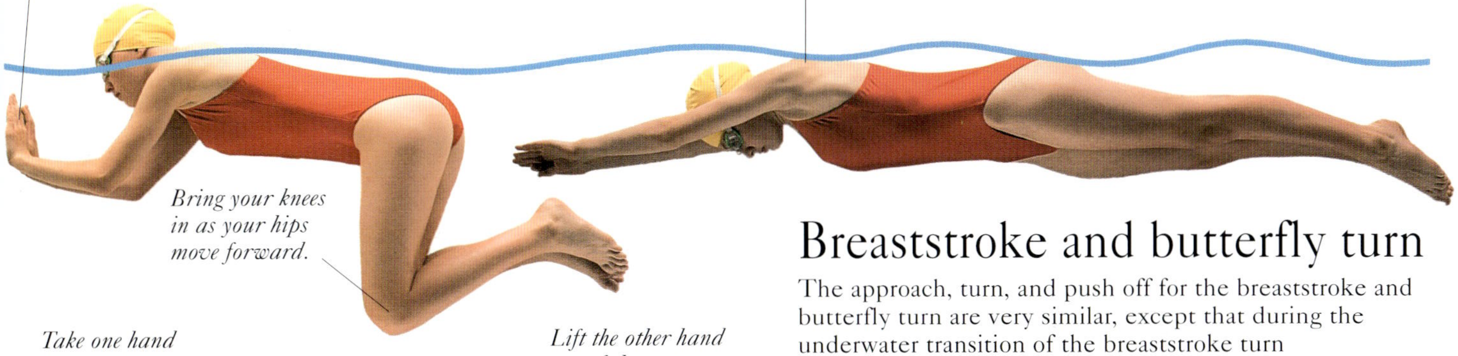

Breaststroke and butterfly turn

The approach, turn, and push off for the breaststroke and butterfly turn are very similar, except that during the underwater transition of the breaststroke turn you are much deeper in the water.

Butterfly approach

On approach, make the touch with your arms almost at full stretch.

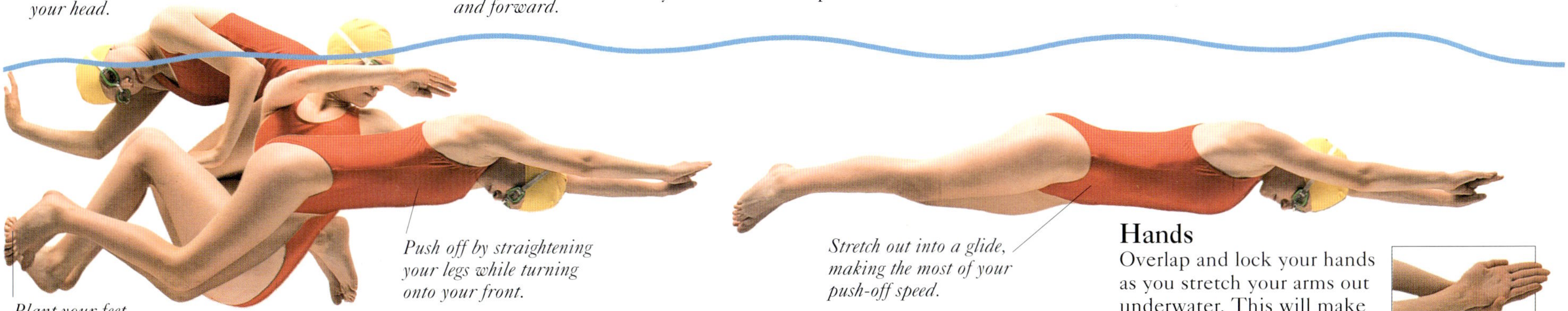

Hands

Overlap and lock your hands as you stretch your arms out underwater. This will make you more streamlined.

Synchronized swimming

IF YOU LIKE swimming, gymnastics, and working out to music then synchronized swimming is the sport for you. If you learn the basic sculls first, you can progress on to making different shapes in the water that are called figures. In time, you will be able to combine the strokes, sculls, and figures and put them to expressive music.

Sculling

Sculling is a very important skill to learn. The movement starts from the shoulder. Sweep the palms of your hands away from your sides, little finger leading, and toward your sides, thumb uppermost. Try to keep your wrists firm, arms straight, and the movement continuous.

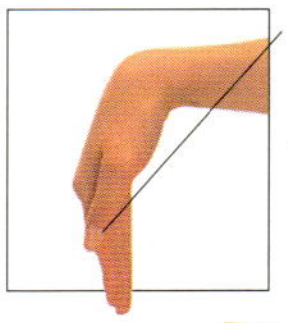

Point your fingers down, flexing from the wrist.

Reverse scull

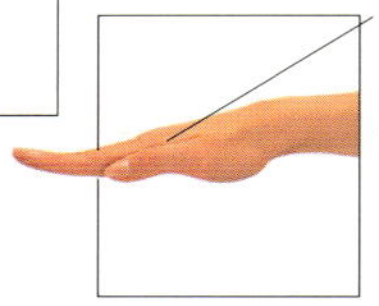

Keep your hands in line with your forearm.

Flat scull

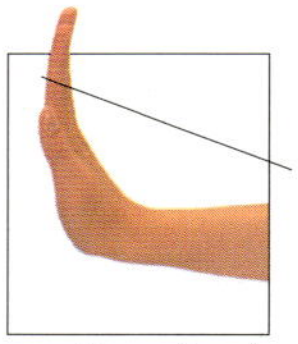

Point your fingers up. Keep your arms close to your body.

Standard scull

Sculling practice

Locking ankles

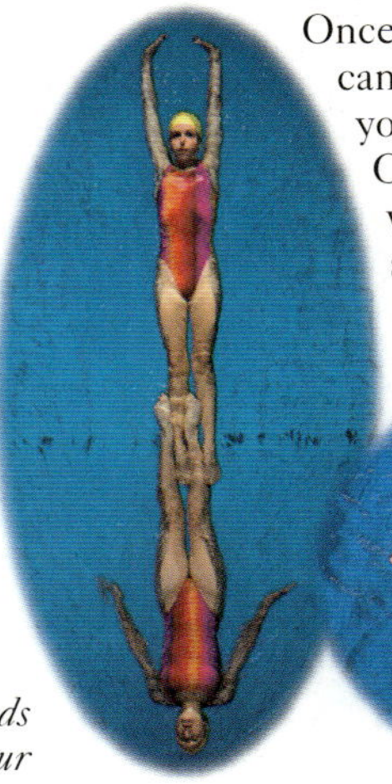

Once you have mastered basic sculling, you can work with a partner. Link feet with your partner, squeezing your legs together. One partner performs a torpedo scull while the other performs a standard scull with their arms at their sides.

Using bottles

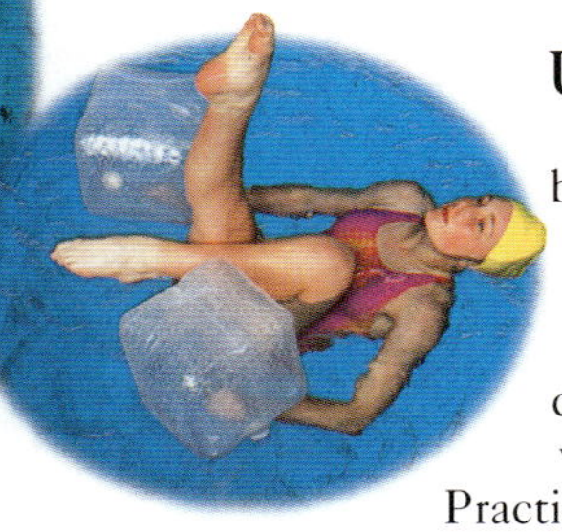

Buoyant plastic bottles will help keep you afloat while learning how to make different shapes with your body. Practice the flamingo position, shown here. Try to keep the extended leg straight.

Canoe scull

To travel headfirst, lie on your front, with your body arched, your hips low, and your chin and feet at the surface. Stretch out your arms, keeping them close to your hips, and use a standard sculling action.

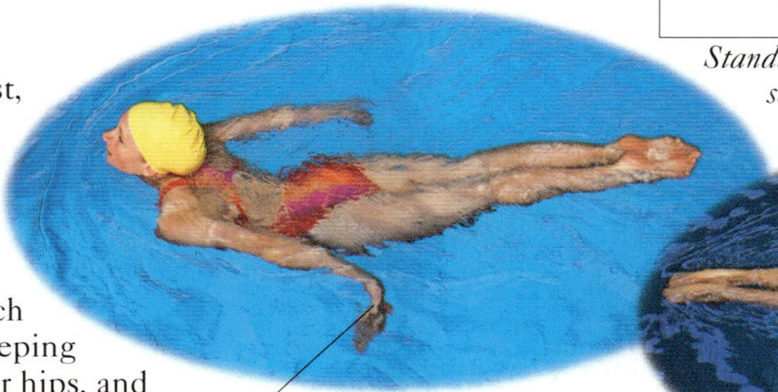

Point your fingers downward.

Torpedo scull

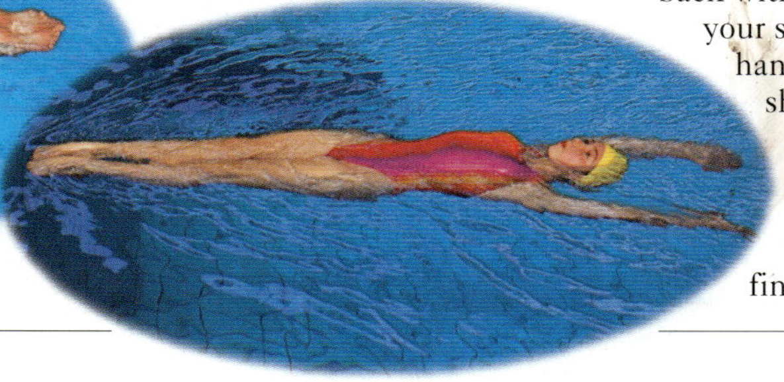

To travel feet first, lie on your back with your legs together, your stomach in, and your hands above your head, shoulder-width apart. Press your arms and hands down into the water and use a standard scull, fingers pointing down.

Figures

A figure is a series of movements. All figures have different names, such as "oyster" and "tub." Once you have mastered good sculling techniques, you can combine these skills to make a sequence of shapes with your body, to create figures.

Oyster

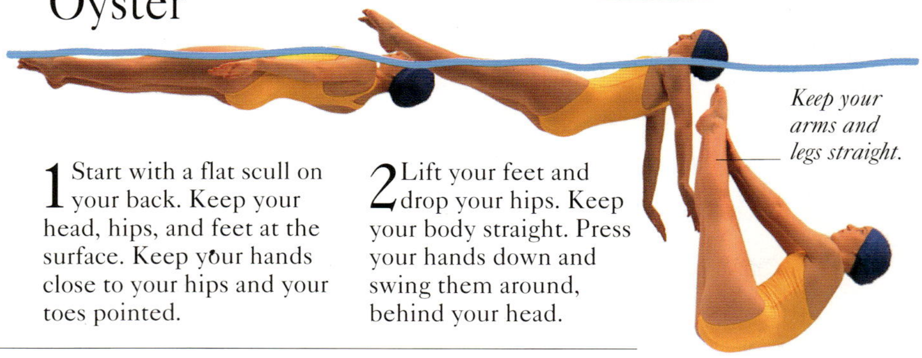

1 Start with a flat scull on your back. Keep your head, hips, and feet at the surface. Keep your hands close to your hips and your toes pointed.

2 Lift your feet and drop your hips. Keep your body straight. Press your hands down and swing them around, behind your head.

Keep your arms and legs straight.

3 Lift your legs up and circle your arms around to touch your ankles.

Hold the oyster position until you are fully underwater.

Tub

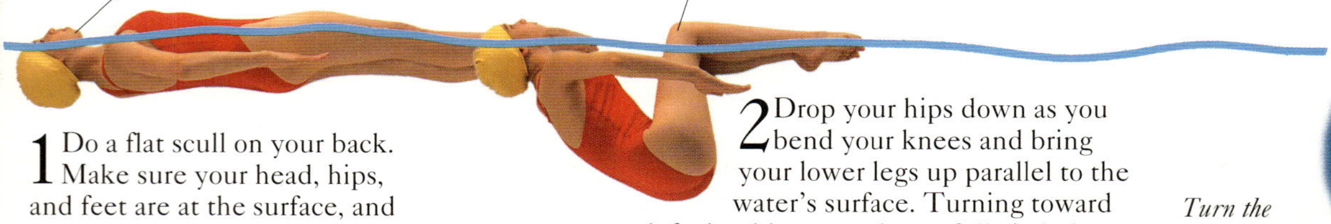

Extend your head back in the water.

Keep your knees above your hips.

1 Do a flat scull on your back. Make sure your head, hips, and feet are at the surface, and scull evenly with your hands close to your hips.

2 Drop your hips down as you bend your knees and bring your lower legs up parallel to the water's surface. Turning toward your left shoulder, complete a full circle by doing a standard scull with your right hand and a reverse scull with your left hand.

Turn the tub figure by sculling with your hands.

Formations

As a synchronized swimmer, you can perform alone, with a partner, or in a group. This gives you the opportunity to make many different kinds of formations. You can use formations both on the water's surface and underwater. It is vital that you have mastered the basic skills before performing formations with other people.

Side bent-knee link

Scull next to your partner, head to toe. Link together by holding each other's ankles close to your shoulder. Bend your outside leg, as shown here and point your toes so that your big toe touches your straight leg. Now do a standard scull with your outside arm to turn headfirst, or a reverse scull to turn feet-first.

Dolphin chain

This formation is performed underwater. Hold your partner's feet with one or two hands. Make sure you keep your body firm, your back arched, and your legs squeezed together. To turn the rotation, scull with one hand while you hold on with the other.

Squeeze your buttock muscles to keep your body arched underwater.

A nose clip will stop water from going up your nose when underwater.

On the surface
A dolphin chain can be performed at the water's surface, too.

Open side bent-knee link

Start with a side bent-knee link. Roll onto your side to face outward and extend and straighten your inside arm. To turn the formation, do a standard scull. You can either keep your heads above or below the water.

Flat sculling will help you hold the cartwheel formation.

Keep your body straight.

Cartwheel

When doing formations in a group, you can make numerous shapes. To make a cartwheel, form a circle. Everyone's left leg should be touching in the middle of the circle. Each person bends their right leg and places it on the hip of the person to the right.

Ballet leg

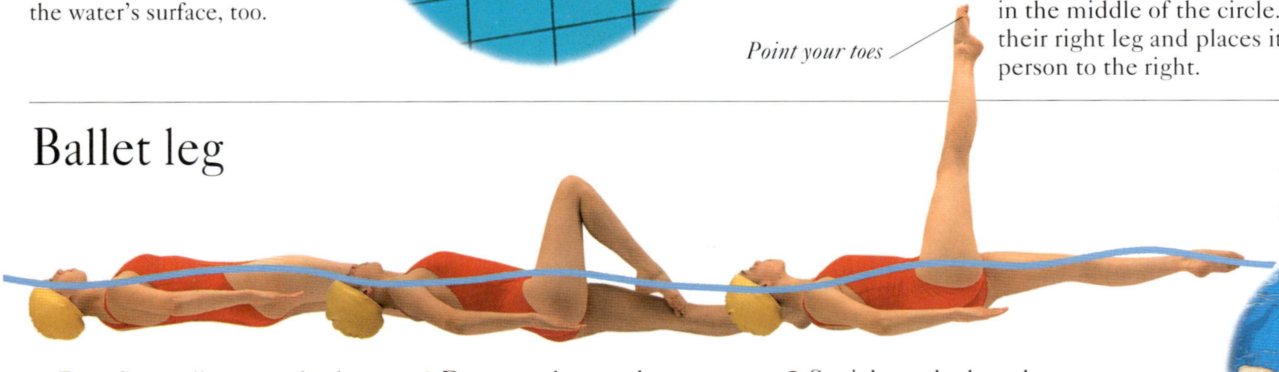

Point your toes

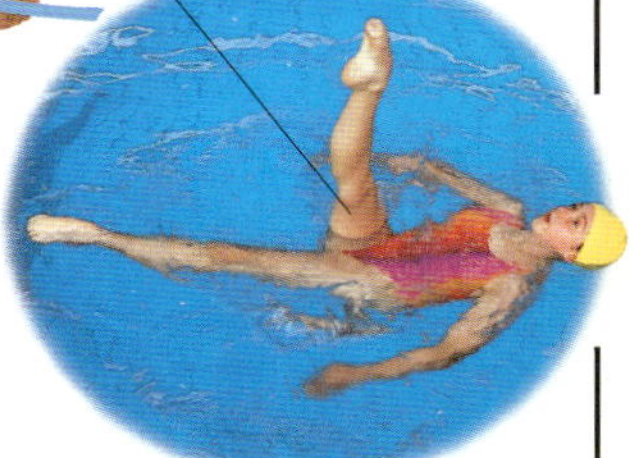

Practice this position with bottles before you try sculling.

1 Do a flat scull on your back. Keep your hips and feet close to the surface. Extend your head, but keep your face above the surface.

2 Draw one leg up along your opposite thigh until your bent thigh is at right angles to your body. Keep the opposite leg straight.

3 Straighten the bent leg and bring it out of the water to make the ballet leg movement. Keep your body and other leg horizontal.

Swimming events and competitions

AS A COMPETITIVE sport, swimming has a very strong following, from local swimming teams through to county, district, national, and international championships, such as the World Championships. Swimming as a sport consists of four areas – swimming, diving, synchronized swimming, and water polo. The international rules are governed by the Fédération Internationale de Natation Amateur (FINA), which has over 160 member countries.

Relay races

There are two types of relay event – the freestyle relay and the medley relay. Each "leg" of the race is completed when the swimmer in the water touches the pool end. The medley relay must be swum in the following order: backstroke, breaststroke, butterfly, and freestyle.

The outgoing swimmer must be ready to leave the block the instant the touch is made.

Medley races

Here, Matthew Dunn of Australia is swimming breaststroke in the individual medley. This event was swum in the Olympics for the first time in 1964.

You need to excel in all four strokes for this event.

The Olympic Games

The Olympics and Paralympics are held every four years, and take place in the same country. In the Paralympics, the swimmers are grouped together according to the level of their disability.

Heats and finals

Heats are swum if there are too many competitors in an event. The winners swim in the final. The fastest has the middle lane, the second and third fastest have lanes on either side, and so on, resulting in the familiar arrowhead, or "V" shape.

Triathlon

The Triathlon is a event in which hundreds of people can compete over long and short courses. The long course involves swimming 2.4 miles (3.8 km), cycling 112 miles (180 km), and running 26.2 miles (42.2 km).

The competitors must move from one event to the next without a break.

An Olympic win

Jeff Rouse won a gold medal for the 100-m backstroke and the 400-m medley relay. at the 1996 Olympics, Atlanta, Georgia.

"Having the gold medal placed around my neck was one of the most fulfilling moments of my life!"

Swim for team medals.

Swimming for gold

As part of a swim team, you will be able to develop your swimming skills through practice and maybe even enter competitions. Your skills will also be useful if you want to take part in other water sports such as canoeing or sailing.

Glossary

During swimming practice, or when watching swimming events, you may find it helpful to understand the meaning of some of the following words and terms.

A

Action Any movement of the limbs in swimming. For every action you perform there is an equal and opposite reaction.
Alternating strokes A term used to describe the crawl.

C

Catch point The point at which the hands start to exert pressure on the water. This occurs soon after the hand(s) enters the water.
Competition pool A pool used for competitions, usually 164 ft (50 m) long. Sometimes there are movable bulkheads and pool floors, so the length and depth can be adjusted.

D

Dolphin kick A double up and down leg kick used when swimming butterfly.
Drag Resistance in the water. A loose swimsuit may cause drag in the water and slow you down.

E

Explosive breathing A breathing technique where air is blown out quickly and forcefully before a new breath is taken.

F

False-start rope A rope used to stop swimmers if the starter decides that a race has started without his or her consent.
Finals The final race of an event that decides the overall winner. The fastest swimmers from the heats (see heats) go forward to the final.
Flip turn A racing turn used to swim crawl.
Freestyle relay A swimming race where four swimmers each swim a leg, or section, using any stroke.
Front paddle A very basic swimming stroke that uses an alternating crawl-style leg kick and a paddling arm action. Also known as "doggie paddle."

G

Glide position A streamlined body position where the arms are outstretched close to the head. A glide can be performed on the water's surface or below it, and on the front or back.
Grab start The most common start in freestyle, breaststroke, and butterfly races. The competitor bends over and presses his or her hands against the starting block to begin the start.

H

Heats A race within an event. When there are more competitors than lanes in an event, the competitors are divided into groups, or heats. Each group swims a heat and the swimmers with the fastest times overall go to the finals.
High-lift style A style of breaststroke used by many swimmers to increase their speed.

I

Intoeing When the feet are turned inward to give greater foot extension and make the foot a more effective paddle.

K

Kickboard Another name for a float. It is usually held in the hands when practicing leg actions.

L

Leg One complete section of a relay race. For example, in a 4 x 100 m relay the 4 team members will each swim 100 m, or one leg, of the race.
Leisure pool A swimming pool specially designed for leisure activities.

M

Medley, Individual An event where competitors perform the following strokes over a set distance: butterfly, backstroke, breaststroke, and freestyle. The freestyle stroke cannot be one of the other three strokes.
Medley, Relay An event where teams of swimmers compete against each other. Each team member swims a different stroke in the following order: backstroke, breaststroke, butterfly, and freestyle. The freestyle stroke cannot be one of the strokes already swum.

P

Pike A position adopted during the flight of some dives, when the swimmer's body momentarily forms an inverted "V" shape.
Prone A swimming position where the swimmer lies on his or her front.
Propulsion Movement through the water as a result of leg or arm action.
Push and glide position A position where the swimmer's body is fully extended so it is

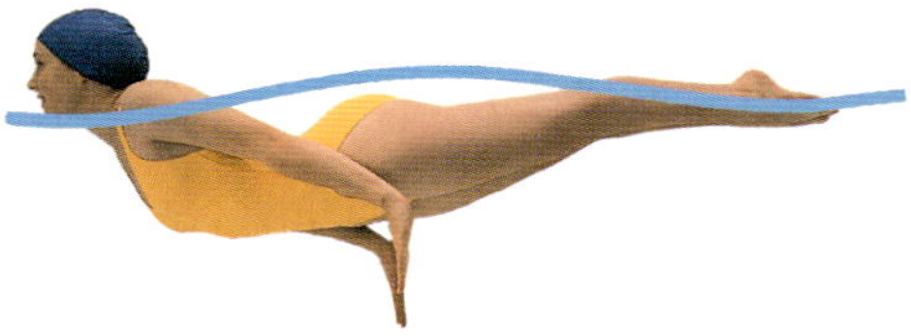

as streamlined as possible. It is used when pushing off from the poolside and gliding through the water.

R

Recovery The stage in a stroke sequence when the swimmer's legs or arms have finished the propulsive stage and are returning to their starting positions.

S

"S" pull An efficient backstroke arm action. The arm makes the shape of an "S" in the water. Also known as the bent arm action.
Screw kick An uneven leg kick used in breaststroke.
Sculling To propel yourself through the water by moving your hands in small figure eight movements.
Simultaneous strokes A term used to describe breaststroke and butterfly.
Supine A swimming position where the swimmer lies on his or her back.
Starting block A block on which swimmers stand to start a race. The block is attached to the poolside and has a nonslip surface.

T

Touch turn A racing turn used when swimming breaststroke and butterfly.
Track start A method of starting a race. The competitor gets into a position with one foot forward and one foot back, and grips the starting block with his or her hands and toes. This start gives a big push off.
Transition The period of time that you are under the water during a start or turn.
Treading water A way of staying afloat in the water. The legs usually perform vertical breaststroke and the arms scull close to the surface.
Trickle breathing A breathing technique where air is released gradually before a new breath is taken.

W

Windup start A start used in relay takeovers, where you build up momentum by circling your arms.

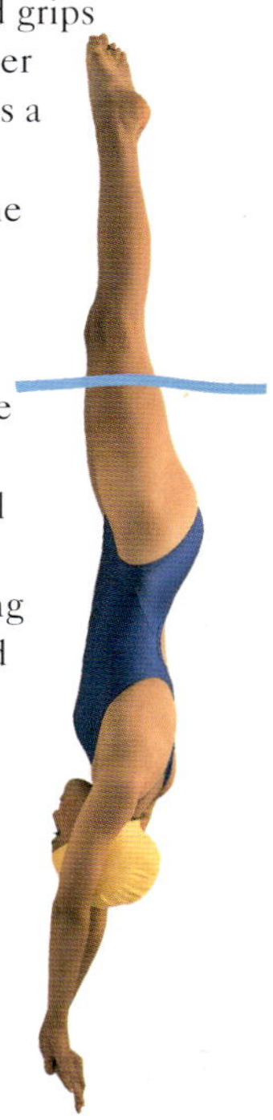

Index

Useful addresses

Here are the addresses of some swimming organizations, which you may find useful.

United States Swimming &United States Olympic Committee on Swimming
One Olympic Plaza
Colorado Springs, CO 80909-5770
ph: 719/578-4578

US Diving
Pan American Plaza
201 S.Capitol Avenue, Suite 430
Indianpolis, IN 46225
ph: 317/237-5252

Synchronized Swimming
US Synchronized Swimming
Pan American Plaza
201 S.Capitol Avenue, Suite 510
Indianpolis, IN 46225

Amateur Athletic Association of the US, Inc.
3206 Prospect, Apt.#45
Cleveland, OH 44115
Attention: Todd Proa
ph: 216/391-6323

American Swimming Coaches Association
301 SE 20th Street
Fort Lauderdale, FL 33316
ph: 305/462-6267

American Red Cross
150 Amsterdam Avenue
New York, NY 10023
ph: 212/787-1000

Acknowledgments

DK would like to thank the following people for their help in the production of this book:

With special thanks to: Rick Cross, for his expert advice at photo sessions and his technical input into the book; the Young Swimmers for their skill, enthusiasm, and hard work; the swimmers' families; Alison Bell for advice on synchronized swimming; Putney Leisure Centre; Brigid Land and Andrew Jackson for assistance on the photo sessions; Hilary Gough (Swimming Development Officer at Wandsworth); Alan Guy and the staff and children at Leander Swimming Club; Clare Brooker for lifeguard duties; Jenny Forest for the use of her pool; Noltan St. Louis; Lesley Betts, Susan St. Louis, Sophia Tampakopoulos, Claire Tindell for design assistance; Patricia Grogan, Sarah Johnston, and Stella Love for editorial assistance; Alison Dunne for the jacket design.

Picture credits
key: B=bottom; L=left; R=right; C=center; T=top; A=above; B=below
Action Plus/Neale Haynes: 13br; /Mike Hewitt: 26cr, 34crb; /Glyn Kirk: 34tr; Allsport/Al Bello: 8tl, 8tr, 34cra; /Shaun Botterill: 26bl; /Simon Bruty: 12-13, 23tr, 25tr, 27br, 29cr; /Michael Cooper: 12bl; /Mike Hewitt 20cl; /David Leach: 12t; /Steve Powell: 34clb; Graham Bool: 34cl; Colorsport: 9bl; /Andrew Cowie 13bl; Mary Evans Picture Library: 9cra; Werner Forman Archive / The British Museum, London: 9t; Dan Helms: 8cl, 8bc, 22cla, 34br; The Image Bank / Gianalberto Cigolini 33clb; Popperfoto: 9cla; US Swimming/Charlie Snyder: 8cr; Speedo: 9br; Sporting Pictures: 30tr; Telegraph Colour Library: 24bl; Topham: 9bc; Alan Towse Photography: 34bl; John Walmsley: 10bl. Jacket: Allsport/Al Bello front bl, back flap; /Tony Duffy back br. End papers: Action Plus/Mike Hewitt.

J.797.2
Rou

Rouse, Jeff
The young swimmer.

CLIFFSIDE PARK PUBLIC LIBRARY, NJ
3 9121 05028586 4